Can I Have This Dance?

Finding Peace in the Tune of the Divine

The Reverend Jeremy L. Williams

Kadeem,

I pray for God's rich blessings in your future! Dream Bigger, Dream Better Dreams,

J.L.W. 2014

For More Copies Contact:
Dream Better Dreams
P.O. Box 402
Huntsville, AL 35804
www.dreambetterdreams.com

DEDICATION

To my mother, Donna Cross Williams, who encouraged me to read twenty books every summer. This is a testament to her faith in God and my education.

CONTENT

ACKNOWLEDGMENTS

This book is the result of opportunities to preach across North Alabama in the nascence of my ministry. From my home church Acklin Chapel C.M.E. Church that continues to provide support and prayers, all the way to local pastors, district officers, and even Episcopal leadership that believed in the potential of a young preacher.

Also, my closest supporters pushed me to greatness. My Mom, younger brother, Tyler, and family are always encouraging and helpful. My closest friends would not allow me to settle for mediocrity. My fraternity line brothers and especially the published poet, Nate Marshall, who show me that achievement is my only option. My mentor, Charles Winfrey, Jr. refuses to let me set my gaze lower than the top. My pastor friend, Adolphus A. Elliott, Sr., has helped me to grow spiritually and gave me the opportunity to preach a bulk of these sermons at the church he serves Gurley C.M.E. My best friend, Dexter Strong, has kept me sharp for the last 9 years as iron sharpens iron. He is the one who said that "your sermons probably make as good of PDFs as MP3s!"

Can I Have This Dance?

Finding Peace in the Tune of the Divine

AN INTRODUCTION

All public speaking is not the same. This is especially true about preaching. For, it is more than reflections from an individual, because the Preacher does not claim to receive her message from tangible resources or personal expertise. However, the claim of the Preacher, especially in the African American context, is drawn from the treasuries of heaven to provide a relevant and timely Word from God!

From that perspective the Preacher is nothing more than the contemporary mouthpiece for an eternally speaking God. Then the message has nothing to do with the Preacher, but it is completely about God and God's message for that present age, world, nation, or community. His message proclaims love to humans even when they are unlovable. His message calls for us to enter into a right relationship with the Divine, which consequently forces us into community with other people. His message informs us of the peace that we have with God through His Son, Jesus Christ.

This peace infiltrates our lives and not only affects our eternal state, but it brings peace into our confused minds and dysfunctional relationships with others. This peace is what God is offering to us when he asks, "Can I have this dance?"

In this book, there are messages through which you can hear that question continually asked. Each message addresses a context and approaches peace from a different point of view. Hopefully, by gleaning from the various messages, one will be able to understand and experience the peace of God in fresh, new ways.

The difference in points of view arise from another peculiarity of preaching. It is alive. It is active. It is audience-driven. From the Hebrew Bible to the Apocalypse of John, God gives messages to contexts and people in line with his global dream for humanity, but that are also specific to the local community (look at Jonah and the Churches in Revelation.) Hence, in this anthology of messages you will see different issues raised and presented, based on how the Preacher discerned God's Word for the congregation. Also, in this work, you will not see the impromptu, unplanned moving of God in the preaching moment (though we attempted to capture some of them.) It's alive!

The title of this book comes from a similar moment of spiritual energy at a Youth and Young Adult Night of an annual conference in Tennessee. The messages "Divine Disturbances," "Silent Treatment," and "Look and Live" all come from messages geared toward inspiring and uplifting congregations to experience the peace of God amidst life's calamities, adversities, and uncertainties. The first chapter of this book, is actually a writing that I did as a part of a series on the Fruit of the Spirit about the characteristics of love based on a work by Donald G. Barnhouse. From which we draw that "Peace is Love, Resting."

This edition of the book also has a bonus chapter, "I've Got to Get My Harvest," which has been added since this book was first published. We also have an excerpt from Jeremy's next book, *From the Frat House to the Church House,* entitled #FollowJesus.

HOW TO READ THIS BOOK

There are a couple of ways that one can read this book.

1. **Read aloud as Sermons.** This works for all of the chapters except for "Peace is Love, Resting." All four of the messages were originally intended to be preached. So, you can preach to yourself, and capture the cadence as the words flow from your lips. The subcategories in each chapter were added for readability, however if you want to read them as sermons, skip over the sections and preach!

2. **40 Day Challenge.** There are forty divisions of this book. Each section and subsection is started by a heading. The Chapter headings are in all caps, the section headings are in small caps and bold, and the subsection headings are in italics. They all range less than five pages. You could slowly digest this book over a forty day period like the disciples tarried for the peace of the Comforter between the Ascension and Pentecost. (When you get done with the introduction, you only have 39 more to go!)

We are not concerned with how you read it, we just want for you to read it so that you can find peace in the tune of the Divine!

CONTEXT OF THIS PREACHER

Though the message is all about God, it has to be translated through us. His message is flawless, but we who deliver the message are full of flaws. Therefore, please disregard any mistakes or errors. I tried to rid this work of them; however, if any remain, please do not allow them to inhibit you from receiving His message.

The way that the Preacher translates the message is via his context. From favorite Scriptures to understanding of words to popular culture, the Preacher is influenced by the world around him. Such influences have shaped this work. I have generated abridged citations of borrowed ideas and quotations.

Noting those two things, I would still like to share Good News with you. This News is so Good, that my craftiness could not dare attempt to proclaim. Nor could the greatest preacher in the world declare. This News is so Good that Jesus Christ Himself preaches it.

How to reach the masses, men of every birth,
for an answer Jesus gave the key
 he said that if I, and I be lifted up from the earth
 will draw all men unto me![1]

Jesus Christ is the great preacher in this volume. So, in this book you should hear his voice declare "Repent." In this work you should hear him say, "The Kingdom of God is at hand." In these messages you should hear him ask, "Can I Have This Dance?"

---

[1] Lift Him Up. By Johnson Oatman, Jr. Online location: http://www.cyberhymnal.org/htm/l/i/f/lifthimu.htm

1 PEACE IS LOVE, RESTING

When peace, like a river, attendeth my way,
When sorrows like sea billows roll;
Whatever my lot, Thou has taught me to say,
It is well, it is well, with my soul.
~Horatio Spafford

Through the Fruit of the Spirit, we are granted the privileged opportunity to peek into the character of God. The same God that declares that "the Lord changes not.[1]" Hence, who God is, was and will be is consistent across the pages of history and throughout the halls of time. The immutability of God is a dynamic feature of the Divine that gives the believer confidence and faith in the one who is

---

[1] Malachi 3:6

"the same yesterday, today, and forever.[1]" For God, who revealed Godself to Moses, as the self-sufficient I AM THAT I AM presents a reality that exists outside of time's "swift transitions naught of earth unmoved can stand—[2]" a reality of a realm that cannot be contained by the temporal nature of this current age; rather, this realm is the eternal epoch that subsumes and brings meaning to this age. It is a sturdy foundation, strong enough for us to build our hopes on, yet fragile enough to sympathize with our expiring existence. This realm is expressed by John as abundant life or life to the full; it is experiencing the very life of God—life without limitation, existence without expiration, essence without cessation.

This is the reality that God's character sustains and reproduces, and by the Spirit of God producing fruit in our lives we are granted access to this realm. A realm where the lion lays down and eats straw with the lamb, where tears have been wiped away and light does not fade at the close of day. A realm where there are no military science classes because there "we ain't gonna study war no more." A realm where the divine rule of God has come, and the Prince of Peace reigns. This is the Kingdom of Heaven! We do not have to wait until "the earthly house of this tabernacle dissolves[3]" to obtain entrance, for Jesus declares that "the Kingdom of God is in the midst of you![4]" We can access this realm now via the Fruit of the Spirit manifested in peace.

In discussing entering the Kingdom through peace, a story comes to mind of hymn-writer Horatio Spafford[5]. Spafford was a successful attorney with a beautiful family. Then, it seems that

---

[1] Hebrews 13:8
[2] Hold to God's Unchanging Hand. By Jennie Wilson. Online Location: http://library.timelesstruths.org/music/Hold_to_Gods_Unchanging_Hand/
[3] 2 Corinthians 5:2
[4] Luke 17:21
[5] See Spaffordhymn.com for more information

tragedy after tragedy occurred in his life, ranging from the Great Chicago Fire destroying much of his wealth to having a child die of scarlet fever. Yet, those events did not end nor climax the catastrophes of his life. The greatest trial came when his family was bound to sail to Europe for a trip. His wife and four children, including a baby daughter, went ahead of him on the Ville du Havre steamer, because he had to attend to some business before he could join them. Then as his family was en route to Europe, another ship struck the Ville du Havre causing the steamer to sink. The crash was so fatal that only 81 of the 307 passengers survived, one of those survivors was Spafford's wife, the only member of his family to be rescued and taken to shore.

At her first opportunity, Mrs. Spafford sent a grim telegram that I am sure it pained her to compose as she sent it to her husband. It read, "Saved alone..." When Horatio Spafford received the telegram, he dropped what he was doing, so that he could support and retrieve his wife. Then as he was on the same sea that had swallowed his children, the captain of the vessel informed Horatio as they sailed over the three-miles-deep area where the Ville du Havre had sunk.

That evening when Horatio was alone in his cabin, the record does not show that he cried out in hopelessness nor does it show that he cursed God, Satan, or his own life. It does not show that grief incapacitated him, or that he gave up on living and religion. But what it does show is that in the quietness of that room, as he was drifting over the ancient enemy of humankind—the sea—these words bled from his heart to provide wells for his pen, "It is well, it is well, with my soul."

Why did Horatio respond like this? He was able to tap into a realm that was able to sustain him when his life was crumbling. Peace attended his way, an incomprehensible peace that passes all understanding. An understanding deeper than knowledge flooded him so that he KNEW that the Prince of Peace had "regarded (his) helpless estate." Hence, the Fruit was able to sustain him; however, the affect of the Fruit (as we've noted earlier) also has a reproducible quality, and Horatio's testimony and song have recreated that moment of peace for others over and over, from single parent mothers who did not know how they were going to provide for their children to students worried about failing to patients learning that they have a terminal disease. For in these moments, we learn that God's love can create eyes of the storm, so that we can rest although everything around us may be in chaos.

SUSTAINING POWER OF PEACE

Focusing on the Rock of Ages

You will keep in perfect peace him whose mind is stayed on you, because he trusts in you. Trust in the Lord forever, for the Lord, the Lord, is the Rock of Ages.
Isaiah 26:3 NKJV

The sustenance of peace nourishes the mind through faith in God. This faith is not misplaced, because it finds itself resting in One who is Faithful. Focusing on God's trustworthiness is essential to obtain and observe the Fruit of Peace. This is a deceptively simple concept that takes a lifetime to master, because there are several aspects that must be accounted for in order to focus on God's faithfulness. I believe that there are two dominant aspects that yield to keeping our mind stayed on the Lord. They are demonstrated in the term "Rock of Ages."

1. Rock…

The image of a rock throughout Scripture is always a reference to the strength and power of the object of the metaphor. For a rock is not a pebble or a stone that we can easily pick up and throw, but rather the picture is that of an immoveable boulder that cannot be compromised and must be navigated around. Therefore, when we can focus our attention on the Sovereign Creator of the Universe, who created everything out of nothing, who adorns Godself with light as with garment, who holds the earth in God's hand, while stretching forth the heavens like a curtain. This is the Great God who destroyed metropolises with fire, blew from God's nostrils and parted a running body of water, rolled the sealed sepulcher's stone away, stopped the sun in the middle of the sky, then on another occasion coerced it to back up. This is the Lord who is the Strength/Rock of my Life of whom shall I be afraid[1]?

If for no other reason, we can trust the Lord, because He is "built God-tough." We can rely on God's strength to keep us. For, a rock could provide a special protection from storms and enemies and wild animals. However, every rock could not provide this special protection. It took a special rock to be able to protect and to keep someone from the perils all around. It took a rock that was cleft. (Herein is what I call Prudential Paradox, because it is the frequent way that God uses means that are counterintuitive to achieve an end. For example, to get you have to give, to reap you have to sow, to be exalted you have to humble yourself.) In the Rock we see a

---

[1] Psalm 27:1

Prudential Paradox, because in order for the Rock to protect you from getting hurt it had to be fissured or split open so that you can get inside. In other words it had to be broken, so you would not be broken. Hence, our Rock of Ages was split, so that we could be whole. Interestingly, peace or *Shalom* (in Hebrew) means completion and wholeness. So, Jesus was broken up, so that you can keep it together. His head was given to a crown of thorns, so that you can keep your mind. He was fractured into pieces so that you could have peace.

> Rock of Ages cleft for me,
> Let me hid myself in Thee.
> Let the Water and the Blood,
> from Thy wounded side, which flowed,
> be for sin double cure.
> Save from wrath and make me pure[1].

2. ...of Ages.

Not only is God the Rock, but God is the Rock of Ages or an eternal Rock. This yields to God's existence outside of time. God is not only a Rock active in our immanent experiences, but God is also standing outside of time orchestrating His plan for our lives. An adage declares of God that, "He may not come when you want Him, but He'll be there right on time." The beauty of the statement shockingly is not in its overt meaning, but there is deeper spiritual undertone to the terse phrase, because it refers to God as "on time." I will argue that it does not really mean that God is punctual, but

---

[1] Rock of Ages. By Augusts M. Toplady. Online location: http://www.cyberhymnal.org/htm/r/o/rockages.htm

rather it means that God exists parallel and on top of time. He works not only in time, but He works on time to fulfill God's purposes. For even when we do not follow the plans that the Lord has laid for us, and when things don't happen and turn out the way we planned, God steps in and on time and reminds us that "all thinks work together for good to those who love God and are called according to His purposes.[1]" As He did with the children of Israel, when their world was falling apart, their families were going to become more dysfunctional, people were going to be killed, and they were going to be led captive. God stepped from on time to in time to declare that "I know the plans I have for you, plans for good and not for evil, plans to prosper you and to give you a hope and future.[2]" So, trust in the Lord! For God, the One who holds the future, is rarely early, never late, but always on time.

So, when we can focus on God as the Rock of Ages, His trustworthiness is overwhelmingly apparent, because He is strong enough to keep our minds in perfect peace. Also, He is on time synergizing or working all things together for our good. When our minds can focus on God, the passage says that God will keep us in perfect peace. When we focus on God's ability, concern, and foresight, we experience peace.

COLLISION OF THE COSMIC AND COMMON

David encouraged himself in the Lord His God. 1 Sam. 30:6 NKJV

That verse comes after David has gone to Ziklag, to fight in a war. Then upon returning to his city, he discovers that the city is burned down and the wives and children of his troops have been

---

[1] Romans 8:28
[2] Jeremiah 29:11

taken captive. His own army is speaking of stoning him; however, David similar to Horatio Spafford, does not cuss them out or talk about how far he brought them. What David does do is encourage himself in the Lord. This act of David finding peace in the midst of turbulent times, vertiginously vocal people and the loss of his own family is miraculous in itself. David brought the cosmic power of God to His situation in the common world, and a consecrated place was forged. For, when the cosmic kisses the common the consecrated is created; when heaven holds hands with the human the holy happens; and when the spiritual sows into the secular the sacred shows up.

Hence, David acknowledges his problem in the common. (The common, human or secular are synonymous for this purpose.) The common is the everyday experience of living. It is breathing, eating, sleeping, going to school, going to work, and regular life. It is marked by the trials that come along with it. It is the real life that we go through and face day by day. It is the upsets, the disappointments, the joys, the victories, the defeats, the whole physical and emotional experience of living in the world. The common represents what it is to be human. This element in David's story is demonstrated in the actual situation occurring. He is faced with people that are supposed to have his back, but when things are not going as well and the weather is not as fair they turn their backs on him. He is faced with his city burned down. It is not the city that he once knew. There are no children playing in the streets, no merchants selling goods. And most painfully his family is taken captive and nowhere to be found. These are not obviously or necessarily spiritual issues. It is the reality that he faces.

Similarly, we face times when reality is difficult to face. The people who are closest to us desert us. The people that swore they would ride with us no matter what, the people that we provide the most for, the people that we would have unquestionably given up our lives for are the ones that are so quickly apt to pick up stones.

Then our cities are burned down by people addicted to drugs and destroying communities. They are burned down by corrupt politicians that do not look out for their constituents. They are burned down by parents that do not take the responsibility to raise their children. Hence, our cities are not safe for our children to even go outside and play. As well, our families are broken down, where single mothers leading families is not the exception but the rule. Young black men are being lead away captive to fill prisons, and young black girls are being led away to unprepared parenthood. This is the common, human and secular.

This bleak reality and presentation of the common is not where the story ends. For David, in spite of the reality in the common, was able to look to another and more meaningful reality— that which originates in the cosmic. David had to take his gaze off of the secular issues that were going on in his life and refocus on the spiritual. For although things were falling apart in the secular realm, in the spiritual realm David could access a place of peace (*shalom*) that was perfectly together, nothing missing and nothing broken. For in that spiritual realm, his God ruled in peace as angels floated on the backs of clouds. And although he did not know the answer, he knew that in that place where Truth resides he could glean a heavenly answer for his human problem.

Then to link these two realms together, David calls for the priest to bring the ephod. The ephod was a common item that was sanctified for divine service just like the priest. For the priest was a human that was selected (either specifically or genetically) by heaven and made holy. Hence, it is fitting that David calls the priest in this meeting of the realms. For what we can see in this picture is David in Ziklag, a common place with secular and human problems, looking up in prayer to the spiritual realm of the heavens under the cosmic rule of God. These two worlds meet at the holy, where heaven high-fives the human in the person of the priest. The entire area where they stand becomes holy ground, because a secular situation seeks guidance from the spiritual, so heaven comes to the human, God comes to earth and humanity's concern goes up to God and the sacred occurs.

In this case for David, God hears David's secular question of "Shall I pursue this band? Shall I overtake them?" then God from the cosmic corridors declares "Pursue; for you shall surely overtake and recover it all." The beauty of God's response is not that it was a message of victory, but rather that it was a message of sureness, because God's word is established in the heavens.[1] So, if it is established in the heavens, humans have to access it through the holy. We access the holy through prayer and praise. This realm of the holy is where David was able to find peace. For although he had no friends in the common, he understood that God was his friend in the cosmic, therefore, he was able to create a consecrated moment and through prayer he was able to encourage himself.

This same method works for us in finding peace. We may not have all the money we want in the secular, but in the spiritual we know that the cattle on a thousand hills[2] belong to the Lord. This brings us peace through the consecrated realm, so that when we worship we can look at both worlds and understand that "my God shall supply all of our needs according to his riches in heaven.[3]" We may have sickness in our human bodies, but when we pray to heaven

---

[1] Psalms 119:89
[2] Psalms 50:10
[3] Philippians 4:19

we see sitting on the right hand of the Father the One that was "wounded for our transgressions, bruised for our iniquities, the chastisement of our peace was upon him, and with his stripes we are healed.[1]" We take these two realms and gain peace in the holy, because we can then understand that those same wounds that were split open centuries ago on Calvary are still relevant to our helpless estate. Then we may have a desire in the common, and we understand that the cosmic law states "seek first the kingdom of God and his righteousness.[2]" The consecrated prayer then gives us peace by informing us that if we "delight ourselves also in the Lord he'll give us the desire of our hearts.[3]"

Peace gives us an avenue to escape from the secular into the sacred. As the world around us moves and changes with uncertainty, we can go into our holy place and gaze into the halls of heaven. Peace is a product of the God-human encounter where their two worlds collide and create a relationship with each other that helps the common to ascend the heights of the cosmic and then return to the human to consecrate it and transform ordinary things into extraordinary things for divine purpose. For it is in the consecrated that God takes his super and adds it to our natural to create the supernatural!

Far away in the depths of my soul tonight
lies a melody sweeter than psalm,
in celestial-like strains it unceasingly falls
o'er my heart like an infinite calm.[4]

---

[1] Isaiah 53:5

[2] Matthew 6:33

[3] Psalm 37:4

[4] Wonderful Peace. By Warren D. Cornell. Online location: http://www.cyberhymnal.org/htm/w/o/wonpeac1.htm

REPRODUCIBILITY OF PEACE

Blessed are the peacemakers, for they will be called children of God.
~Jesus

The amazing power of fruit, especially the Fruit of the Spirit is their ability to reproduce. Jesus' statement infers that a powerful inner peace has already come upon the peacemaker. For not only have they gone into the realm where they are virtually unaffected by what goes around, but they can transform the environment around them to one of completeness. They can take war tattered remains and insurgent attacks to produce peace or *shalom* (which also means welfare, health, tranquility and prosperity).   They are given the epitaph of "children of God," because like their father they can create something out of nothing, safety out of shots, friendship out of fighting, and tranquility out of trifling people.

The peacemaker and the warrior are very similar. The main similarity is that the peacemaker and the warrior are operating not on behalf of themselves. They both operate on behalf of a cause that is greater than themselves and that will exist with or without them. However, the difference between the two surfaces in their theaters of battle. The warrior fights in a field that was created for him and is limited by someone else's creation. But on the other hand the peacemaker makes or creates the field that he operates in to make peace; hence the peacemaker's power is limitless. For Paul declares, in speaking of the Fruit of the Spirit "against such there is no law.[1]" Peace cannot be limited. One cannot create a legislation strong enough to stifle the creation of peace although conventions and generals can limit and cease war.

---

[1] Galatians 5:20

The reason why it cannot be legislated is for the fact that reproduction of peace is effortless. One does not have to carry placards and signs to create a peaceful environment. All you have to do is enter into your realm of peace, and the atmosphere around you will change. Like all fruits, within it is seed that must be sown in order to reproduce. Yet, in another Prudential Paradox we note that fruit are sweet so that they can be eaten by ravenous animals and excreted, fertilized to then reproduce. So, as the fruit sustains the eater its seed is preparing itself to be sown. Similarly, environments of doubt, depression, and despair surround us frequently to consume us. It seems that our peace is being digested, our holy place is sacrileged, and our consecrated space desecrated as the jaws of jealousy, mandibles of misery, and teeth of trial chew on our peace. The victory is that the vicious attempts to destroy our peace are actually fertilizing its seed so that our peace can be reproduced. Although the seed has to go through the disgusting situation, it cannot be broken down by stomach acid or digestive juices; as a matter of fact, it was made to go through them. The seed of our peace cannot be broken, although the flesh of the fruit may be devoured, the seed cannot be broken! The seed is built to go through the muck and the mire so that it can produce more of the DNA that it holds securely.

Hence, the Prudential Paradox is that the seed that must be sown, it is not sown by the peacemaker, but it is sown by the peace snatcher. The peace snatcher is the enemy of the peacemaker that tries to destroy their peace only to realize that their war, aggressiveness, and belligerence actually only helped to further your peace. The duty of the wind and of the enemy is to shake the seed loose, so that at the end of the day you can spring up in more places than if you had not been attacked. Your peace can manifest itself not just when you're all alone but when people are lying on you. It can spring up not only when things are going well, but when things are going terrible. It can rise up not only in your life, but in the life of others who jeered and joked about you being calm when turbulence was all around. Therefore, in those situations that had come to destroy, they were just the opportunity for your peace to reproduce.

"What you (peace snatchers) meant for my evil. God used it for my good.[1]"

SABBATH IN THE SEA

Peace, be still. ~ Jesus

In Mark 4, we see Jesus and his disciples sailing across the sea and a windstorm arises that begins to swamp the boat. However, despite all of this commotion around him, Jesus rests on the cushion in the stern of the ship. The disciples are shocked at this realization, but as for us outside of the story, it should not be remarkable that Jesus was asleep in the midst of such an exciting time. For Jesus the Son of God, in this instance easily resembles his Father, who after creating the world with things in motion for only six days decides that it is naptime.

In Genesis, when God decides to rest on the seventh day, God rests big by creating an institution—the Sabbath. Although work could not be done on this day it was essential to prosperity (*shalom*, peace), because the Ancient Israelites that adopted this practice participated in another Prudential Paradox. For in the Sabbath, rather than losing a day of labor, they gained a week of

---

[1] Genesis 50:20

productivity. Their week was not empty because they did not work on the Sabbath, but their week was complete because they could rest in the likeness of God. The Sabbath day sanctified their week, the Sabbath month sanctified their year, the Sabbath year sanctified their decade, and the Sabbath of years (year of Jubilee) sanctified their semi-centennial. In other words, the Sabbath sanctified their lives. By resting, they gained God's faithful and unresting vigilance over them.

Why did they gain this special favor? I believe the author of Hebrews would argue that, "God is a rewarder of those that diligent seek him[1]" and "without faith it is impossible to please him." God rewarded them, because the Sabbath is an act of faith. Resting and not relying on our own ability to provide for ourselves allows us to observe God operating while we have clocked out and gone home. Resting or Sabbath allows us to see God working on our behalves, and it forces us to stay out of the way to regain strength for when God wishes for us to be co-workers with God. We don't have to just experience Sabbath on our day designated to worship; however, we can experience it when we take 10 minutes or an hour to just rest and "lift up our eyes unto the hills.[2]" Take a Sabbath break in the morning or during the day to just talk to God and watch how your day is blessed from sacrificing such a small amount of time. Sabbath is the ultimate sign of faith. Note when one is sleeping they cannot take care of themselves, they are completely defenseless, but when we rest in God, although we are sleeping we are trusting in the One "that neither slumbers nor sleeps![3]"

"I will both lie down and sleep in peace; for you alone, O LORD, make me lie down in safety.[4]"

---

[1] Hebrews 11:6
[2] Psalm 121:1
[3] Psalms 121:4
[4] Psalms 4:8

In Mark 4, we can see this Sabbath principle in full operation in the life of Jesus. For though the billows were rising and the wind was pounding, Jesus could rest. Mark records that he was resting on a cushion or pillow, but if I could use my sanctified imagination and peer into the spiritual realm, Jesus was resting on the promises of God. When the ship began to reel and rock like a drunken man, he may have remembered that "he that dwelleth in the secret place of the most high shall abide under the shadow of the Almighty.[1]" When darkness was surrounding the ship, it may have come to mind, "The LORD is my light and my salvation.[2]" Then when the disciples, people that were supposed to be close to him, came barraging him with questions, he may have meditated on when "my mother and father forsake me, then the LORD will bear me up.[3]" Regardless, on what he was resting, he was taking a Sabbath. Then this passage supports that a Sabbath is a faith thing, because Jesus asks, "Have you still no faith?" Faith to rest in a God who loves you. Faith to have peace in the midst of the storm. Or the most powerful aspect, faith to speak peace to the storm.

What Jesus does is take the peace, *shalom*, rest that he has received from God that created a personal Sabbath, and as the Prince of Peace, reproduces the peace that he has on the inside of him by speaking into the situation. This word of peace then reminds the sea of the cosmic time when God Himself had spoken to the infant world and declared Sabbath. The sea then subsides, because Jesus' *shalom* reminds the wind and the sea of the pre-lapsarian peace, that the creation is groaning for. It is for this peace, that the Apostle Paul declares that all of creation is groaning for the children of God to appear. So, although we have peace like a river, it is imperative that

---

[1] Psalms 91:1
[2] Psalms 27:1
[3] Psalms 27:10

we recreate peace all around us, because your job does not like to be in confusion, it is looking for peace. Your family does not desire to be dysfunctional, it is seeking Sabbath. Your community is not content with poor education and outrageous violence, it is looking for rest. Your job, your family, your community and for that matter all of creation is listening for your "Peace, be still."

CONCLUSION

Peace is a powerful Fruit that if we can allow it to grow and reproduce in our lives, it will sustain us through difficult and joyous times. By focusing on the Rock of Ages we can experience the collision of the cosmic that creates a place for us to escape the uncertainties and turbulences of this world. As well, we can reproduce this Fruit as the children of God noting that as JFK stated (and I paraphrase) the Chinese word for crisis has two characters, one meaning danger and the other meaning opportunity. So when the peace-snatcher comes to destroy our peace, we understand that it is an opportunity for our peace to grow like never before. Then as our peace grows up in us, we can rest knowing that God is watching over us to protect us as we experience a Sabbath within ourselves. Then we can speak to situations and circumstances to recreate the Sabbath all around us.

Peace! Peace! Wonderful peace,
coming down from the Father above,
sweep over my spirit forever, I pray,
In fathomless billows of love.[1]

---

[1] Wonderful Peace. By Warren D. Cornell. Online location: http://www.cyberhymnal.org/htm/w/o/wonpeac1.htm

2 DIVINE DISTURBANCES

Revelation 1:**9-11**-20; 4:1 NRSV

I, John, your brother who share with you in Jesus the persecution and the kingdom and the patient endurance, was on the island called Patmos because of the word of God and the testimony of Jesus. [*] [10]*I was in the spirit* [*] *on the Lord's day, and I heard behind me a loud voice like a trumpet* [11] *saying, 'Write in a book what you see and send it to the seven churches, to Ephesus, to Smyrna, to Pergamum, to Thyatira, to Sardis, to Philadelphia, and to Laodicea.'*

Have you ever been disturbed? You had one plan, but something interrupted it? You may have been working on a project and somebody calls, texts, or pop chats you on facebook? If you have then you can understand what's going on in this passage, because something similar is going on in the spiritual realm.

Many times people have an apprehension to the book of Revelation, because of its rich symbolism that may be difficult to interpret, and its subject matter that's understandably complicated to comprehend. We frequently feel that we cannot connect or possibly we do not wish to connect with this book outside of the "number that no man could number[1]" and the vision of the New Jerusalem. However, I would submit to you to rethink this book under the auspices of the advice given to Timothy that "all Scripture is given by the inspiration of God and is profitable for doctrine, reproof, correction, and instruction in righteousness.[2]" Hence, because this is God breathed, it is a revelation not just to John the Revelator and the seven churches in Asia in the first century, but this is an apocalyptic unveiling of knowledge hidden from the foundation of the world for you in the 21st century. This type of revelation only comes when God interrupts.

I would like to use John's experience as one that is analogous to the contemporary reader of this passage. For, as John was greeted on the Isle of Patmos by a divine disturbance, so can those that listen to this message and people everywhere experience when God interrupts. God has plans to interrupt your life, if God hasn't already. Even if God already has, God is getting ready to interrupt it again. Therefore, if God is setting your date for a divine disturbance it is

---

[1] Revelations 7:9
[2] 2 Timothy 3:16

24

probably useful to know the definition, qualifications for, and purpose of a said disturbance.

THE DEFINITION OF AN INTERRUPTION

First, let us define what it means to be interrupted by God. It is the cosmic cataclysm when the Sovereign of the Universe enters into our presence. For we understand that during praise, prayer, and other means of worship we ascend the lofty hill of the mountain of God and enter into God's holy, holy, holy[1] presence making us holy. However, when God interrupts, God enters into our presence and everything around us becomes holy. Our families, our jobs, our relationships, our grades, and our athletics all become holy, because the nature of being in the presence of God transforms ordinary things into instruments for extraordinary purposes. This is the meaning of holiness, it's not as mystical as we tend to believe, rather it is taking natural things and adding God's super to them to make them supernatural. By something being supernatural it is different, it is called out, it is separated, it is sanctified.

It is a disturbance, because frequently it changes our plans and swaps them with God's plans. But we should not worry, because Jeremiah declared, "I know the plans I have for you declares the Lord. Plans for good and not for evil plans to give you a hope and an expected end.[2]"

God breaks into our lives to make them holy by various means. One may ask, how can God break into our lives and God is

---

[1] Holy, Holy Holy. By Reginald Heber. Online location:
http://www.cyberhymnal.org/htm/h/o/holyholy.htm
[2] Jeremiah 29:11

everywhere? That's a great question. God does so by manifesting in ways that arrest your attention.

Frequently, God does not directly cause the situation for God's breaking in, but God comes into our everyday lives filled with scandal, sin, and shame, but that does not hinder Him. For example, as we drive down the highway, we believe that God is protecting us, but when we lose control of our vehicle and would have been killed by a passing 18-wheeler and something guides us, that's a divine disturbance and your car becomes the site of a miracle. You know that Jesus said that he would always be with you, but when you studied all night for a test and still could not grasp the information, but when the test came, things started to make sense that did not before, and you don't understand how you understand the questions. That's when God interrupts, and that test has become God's sanctuary. When you are in a relationship that you know is not good for you but you continue to try to make work, but it will not. That is a divine disturbance and your singleness is sanctified. Even catastrophic disasters like the earthquakes in Haiti[1] (don't get me wrong I will not argue that God caused them) God interrupted and sent in aid from churches like Gurley[2] and all over the world to demonstrate the love of God; hence transforming Haiti into Holy Ground. Holy Ground like the desert soil surrounding the burning bush in Sinai's desert that was not consumed and called out to Moses as he was herding Jethro's sheep, "This is a public service announcement and a divine disturbance. take off your shoes, because your standing on Holy Ground!"

This leads us to John in our text, exiled for the word of God and the testimony of Jesus Christ, but God breaks into his Patmos

---

[1] Reference to tragic, infamous earthquakes that occurred in 2010
[2] The Church where this message was delivered.

solitary confinement in the Person of the Son of Man declaring that "'I am the Alpha and the Omega. The beginning and the end. I am he, who lived, was dead, and behold I am a live forever more![1]" And if you don't mind, John, let me interrupt you for a little while." Now that I've defined it; have you ever had a divine disturbance?

A Simpler Definition

Maybe somebody was lost in my jargon, let me explain it like the seasoned saints would, when you should have been dead sleeping in your grave, but God interrupted and made death behave. That's a divine disturbance. Or maybe the psalmist described the divine disturbance the best when he penned, "If it had not been for the Lord on my side, when my haters rose up against me they would have swallowed me up![2]" However, "when the enemy came in like a flood, the Lord interrupted and raised up a standard.[3]" The songwriter said that "when I was down to my last dime,

Jesus (interrupted and) came in right on time.[4]"

Perhaps the hymnologist wrote it best,

"I was sinking deep in sin
far from the peaceful shore.
Very deeply stained within
sinking to rise no more,
but the master of the sea (interrupted and)
heard my despairing cry.

---

[1] Revelation 1:18
[2] Psalms 124: 1
[3] Isaiah 59:19
[4] A favorite African American expression of the Providence of God

And from the waters lifted me.

Now safe am I![1]"

Has anybody been disturbed by the divine?

REQUIREMENTS FOR A DISTURBANCE

Second, we need to discuss the requirements for God to interrupt someone. Upon my first reading of this passage in the parameters of this message, I thought that because John, according to conservative theologians was a Son of Thunder. he was the beloved disciple that etched the eagle-eyed gospel, who laid his head on Jesus' chest at the Last Supper. I thought that he was the one that worked tirelessly in Ephesus equipping the saints, and even after his departure he was so concerned with them that he wrote three letters to his "little children.[2]" I thought that it was this preaching John who in the face of the oppressive Roman government would not turn his back on Christ; therefore, tradition states that they boiled him in hot oil, but the Lord would not let him fry like a KFC double-down sandwich. So, the only way that they could rid themselves of him was by sending him to an island where his message could not reach anybody. That's who I thought that this John in our text was; hence, it logically follows that this John fulfills the requirements whatever they are to be interrupted by God.

However, I discovered that this did not fit the pattern of divine disturbances throughout Scripture. I knew like many of you know, that "our minds are not God's mind. And as the heavens are

---

[1] Love Lifted Me. By James Rowe. Online Location:
http://www.cyberhymnal.org/htm/l/l/lliftdme.htm
[2] Standard Johannine address to the believing communities to which he wrote

far above the earth, even so are God's thoughts above our thoughts.[1]" With this in mind, upon further research I discovered that there is another school of thought on the identity of this John. Rev. Elliott, they do not say what color his shoes are,[2] but they bring into light that John was a popular name, and nothing links this John with the John of the gospel and the letters, hence this John is virtually a nobody. He does not have the qualifications of the apostle, nor does he have a degree in theology, he hasn't necessarily been preaching for several years. We don't know much about this John, but what we do know is that he was in the Spirit on the Lord's Day and God interrupted him. God interrupting him is what qualified him.

The Only Qualification

It does not matter about your background, where you come from, what you've done in your past, or even what you may be doing now, how many times you've been married, how many times you've failed God, others and yourself. It does not matter how much money you have or don't have. You don't need anything for God to interrupt you. **God does not interrupt people who are qualified, God qualifies those God interrupts!** Amos could testify to this, he would say, "I was not a prophet nor was I a prophet's son. I was a herdsman and a gatherer of sycamore, (but I was disturbed by the Divine!)[3]"

---

[1] Isaiah 55:8-9

[2] A running joke between Pastor Elliott and I about the value of biblical scholarship, and one of his catch-phrases is that "we don't have to know what color John's shoes are to understand the Scriptures relevance to us."

[3] Amos 7:14

The text tells us that it was the Lord's Day. Knowing that the Lord's Day is Sunday, because it is the day for traditional Christian worship. John may have been having worship service by himself, and somewhere between the call to worship and the benediction. Maybe it was before the invocation, maybe it was after the offering, possibly it was during a selection but sometime on the Lord's Day, God interrupted him. It seems to me that that places us at the right place at the right time for God to interrupt our lives and transform them into something for God's glory.

Another thing we can gather from the text is that due to John's exile, he was by himself. You may wonder why you don't fit in. You may wonder why you think differently, and why people don't seem to understand you. You may wonder why you can't be like everybody else. It is because you are being positioned for a divine disturbance. Sometimes God cannot disturb you because you have too many other people disturbing you! It's ok to turn off your cell phone, and get off facebook so that you can be disturbed by the Divine. But whether you exile yourself or not God knows how to get your attention, because there is no requirement for a divine disturbance. Look at Paul, he was not alone and he definitely was not in a worship service, but between Jerusalem and Damascus he was interrupted by the Son of God. This demonstrates that whether you think you're the highest saint or the "chief of sinners[1]" God can and will interrupt you!

---

[1] 1 Timothy 1:15

PURPOSE OF A DISTURBANCE

To Go Higher

We have defined a divine disturbance. We have given the requirements for a divine disturbance. This leaves us with the third point—the purpose. God disturbs us so that God can take us higher. By being interrupted by God, John was able to enter an open door into heaven. Likewise, when God interrupts us, God leaves the door open in heaven so that we can follow God to higher heights. "For we are seated with Christ in heavenly places.[1]" God is trying to take us higher. The places that God can take us are beyond our wildest imagination, because "eye has not seen, ear has not heard, nor has it entered into the heart of man what God has for those whom God has disturbed and love Him.[2]" But remember that when God interrupts, He consecrates everything around us, and as we go higher we are following what Isaiah called the Highway of Holiness. God wants you to know that there is more that you can do for Him. You cannot stay where you are after you have been interrupted by God. When God comes down to us, God pulls us up to Him.

To See Jesus in a New Way

By virtue of us going higher we get to see the second reason that God interrupts. God disturbs us so that we can see Jesus in a new way. The higher we get, the closer we can see Jesus, and sometimes we need a close up. Regardless of how much we know about Jesus or think we know about Jesus there is still a lot to learn. John in the text

---

[1] Ephesians 2:6
[2] 1 Corinthians 2:9

sees Jesus as never before decked in garb as the Son of Man. Biblically, we can see account after account of who Jesus is. For it is the goal of the Gospel to understand who Jesus is. That's why all of the Evangelist of the New Testament have a way that they see Jesus.

Matthew would say that He's God's Teacher.

Mark would say that He's God's Preacher.

Luke would say that He's God's Son.

John would say that He's God's Word

Paul would say that He's God's Savior.

Peter would say that He's God's Christ.

James would say that He's God's Prophet.

The Revelator would say that He's God's Lamb.

That's great and solid, but after a divine disturbance the Gospel has an even more powerful resonance. Hence, I pose to you the same question that Jesus posed to Peter in the plain of Caesarea Philippi. "Who do you say that I am?[1]" It takes a divine disturbance in order to answer this question for ones self. How do I know this? Because when the disciples told Jesus who other people said that he was, he was unsatisfied. However, when Peter gave the correct answer in Matthew, Jesus said, "Blessed art thou Simon Bar-jonah for flesh and blood has not revealed this unto to you, but my Father in heaven divinely disturbed you."

I can attest to this personally. For though I know Isaiah 53:5 is true, it takes God interrupting my life during a sickness or illness to

---

[1] Matthew 16:13-20

say that He was wounded for MY transgressions, bruised for MY iniquities, the chastisement of MY peace was upon him and with his stripes I am healed. Although I understand how Ephesians says that we are saved by grace through faith, it took the divine disturbance of me realizing how my sins offended God that I could say, "Amazing grace how sweet the sound that saved a wretch like me.[1]" I understood that many are called but the laborers are few, but it took a divine disturbance of realizing that people are not living up to their potential that I could self-actualize Charles Wesley's words "A charge to keep I have and a God to glorify. A never dying soul to save and fit it for the sky![2]" It's something about when you know for yourself, with a divine disturbance, that you do not need anybody else's approval. You know for yourself. When John saw the one with a robe down to his feet with hair white like wool, eyes of fire, and tongue of a two-edged sword, he did not need anybody to tell him that God is real. He could stand along with Paul who said, "I know in whom I have believed![3]"

To Interrupt Others

God interrupts us to interrupt others. When John was interrupted by God he was immediately given a group to share his experience with—the seven churches of Asia. Similarly, when God interrupts us and takes us higher and allows us to see Jesus in new ways, we should share it with somebody. As a matter of fact, according to Romans you can only be saved after you confess with

---

[1] Amazing Grace. By John Newton. Online Location:
http://www.constitution.org/col/amazing_grace.htm
[2] A Charge to Keep I Have. By Charles Wesley. Online location:
http://www.cyberhymnal.org/htm/c/h/chargkeep.htm
[3] 2 Timothy 1:12

your mouth "the Lord Jesus." With this in mind I will interrupt you with my divine disturbances. Rev. Elliott asked me to speak on why I am the way I am. I have to say that it is, because I have a had a divine disturbance. God broke into my life and transformed the very way that I see the world.

He sanctified my perspective so that the way I see the world is not from the view of this age. God disturbed me when I was just reading the Bible, God spoke to me and showed me that there is power for the believer. We don't have to be victims of our circumstances and life situations. Christ has set us free. God interrupted my life to let me know that "greater is he that is in me than he that is in the world.[1]" "I am the head and not the tail, above and not beneath, the lender and not the borrower. My enemies come at me in one way and depart in seven.[2]" Hence, by knowing who I am in Christ, which was confirmed by a divine disturbance, I am confident in who I am and whose I am. My goal is to share this confidence with everybody. Although it may not all always be easy, God is able to do "exceedingly and abundantly above all that I can ask or think by the power that works in me.[3]" Therefore, like John after he saw heaven for himself, he did not need anybody to confirm it for him; we can declare

"Blessed assurance, Jesus is mine.
O what a foretaste of glory divine.
Heir of salvation purchase of God
born of his spirit washed in his blood.[4]"

---

[1] 1 John 4:4
[2] Deuteronomy 28
[3] Ephesians 3:20
[4] Blessed Assurance. By Fanny J. Crosby. Online Location: http://www.hymnsite.com/lyrics/umh369.sht

This is because God interrupted me and took me to heights that I could not even imagine. Because of this experience God led me to explain to people who they are in Christ and more importantly who Christ is in them. I pray that God interrupting me has interrupted you and inspires you to interrupt somebody else.

3 SILENT TREATMENT

Exodus 14:1-**10-14**-31 NRSV

As Pharaoh drew near, the Israelites looked back, and there were the Egyptians advancing on them. In great fear the Israelites cried out to the Lord. [11]They said to Moses, 'Was it because there were no graves in Egypt that you have taken us away to die in the wilderness? What have you done to us, bringing us out of Egypt? [12]Is this not the very thing we told you in Egypt, "Let us alone and let us serve the Egyptians"? For it would have been better for us to serve the Egyptians than to die in the wilderness.' [13]But Moses said to the people, 'Do not be afraid, stand firm, and see the deliverance that the Lord will accomplish for you today; for the Egyptians whom you see today you shall never see again. [14]The Lord will fight for you, and you have only to keep still.'

Believe it or not, I used to get in trouble. I generally got in a particular kind of trouble. It wasn't that I had violated a rule, misbehaved in school, or broke the law. It was not trouble with my hands or with my feet, but it was trouble with my mouth. My mother had a very particular tactic to use for me when I either talked too much or said something disrespectful. Outside of those times she popped me in the mouth, she used this sagacious strategy known as the silent treatment where she ignored what I said and acted as if what I said was unimportant. This hurt more than a physical touch, because it in effect forced me to swallow my syllables to the point where I had to regurgitate an apology. This strategy was effective for her on me, and as I matured I learned that it was effective for me on others. For some reason, I realized that it has this unparalleled path to slide beneath the skin of young ladies, but I won't go there today.

What I do want to submit to you is that this system has the power to give you victory over your enemies, power over your situations, and strength over your weaknesses. In this message are keys that will help you reduce deadly stress, keys that will give you agency where you feel impotent, and keys that will unleash the military force of the Yahweh Sabaoth, the Lord of Hosts, the Lord of armies, who wants to fight all of your battles for you. He wants you to cheerlead as He leads the charge on your behalf. He doesn't need for you to scream to the top of your lungs, He doesn't need for you to shout your voice out or bust somebody's eardrum. All He really needs from you is silence.

Yes, the silent treatment is the solution to conquering our Egyptian enemies, watery woes, and depressing darkness. Though it seems improbably simple, it is inconceivably complex. Especially in a society where we go to sleep listening to musical lyrics, wake up hearing television programs, work out wearing Beats headphones, and drive around talking on Androids and iPhones. When was the last time that we experienced silence? We have been conditioned to believe that every moment needs to be filled with excitement, conversations, sounds, noise, or speech. Even in our worship services it has become our practice that someone needs to be singing something, praying something, preaching something, or doing something, because we don't want to fall victim to that awkward silence. It is in our constantly being busy, we find ourselves subject to the acronym that some would say that busy stands for—bound under satan's yoke. Today, I want to make an argument for the awkward silence, because in the silence we can reflect on ourselves as who we are and not as who we pretend to be, in the silence we transform secular minutes into sacred moments, in silence we avail our hearts to clearly hear the voice of God. "The Lord is in His holy temple, let all of the earth keep silence before Him.[1]"

Rev. McDuffie once explained to me that that verse is intentional in its phraseology. It says *silence* not *silent* for a reason. For we do not want you to be confused this morning and take away that God is calling for you to be mute, to not say syllables, to lock your lips, and be silent. Rather, we are compelling you to posture your head, heart, and hope in a direction towards God and live in silence from the quakes of life's uncertainties and the winds of inevitable defeat and the shadows of hopelessness. Yes, silent is an adjective that describes points in time, but silence is a state of being. And it takes silent moments to bring your being into an orchestral, harmonious silence with the Divine.

The Sabbath reflects silence. For it gives us a picture of resting without concern, care or consequences. It captures a moment when there is no work, because God has done it all. There is no need,

---

[1] Habakkuk 2:20

because God has provided it all. There is no stress, because God has calmed it all. And there is no lack, because God has filled it all. This tranquil time is not lost in ancient memories, but it is available to all of us every day of our lives, and not just on Sundays. For we have been granted access by the One who claimed to be the Lord of the Sabbath. The one who declares, "Come unto me all you who labor and are heavy laden and I will give you rest. Take my yoke upon you and learn of me, for my yoke is easy and my burden is light![1]" He wants to inject these moments into our lives and bring us into beautiful silence by means of the silent treatment.

Friends, it is indeed a treatment, so, we must look at the symptoms that would compel such a treatment. Come with me to verse 11.

Here we find the Children of Israel who have been given coerced permission from Pharaoh to leave the bondage of Egypt to worship the Lord. However, after Pharaoh's heart is hardened again he gets all of the chariots, chariot drivers, army, navy, marines, air force, and coast guard of Egypt and chases the Children of Israel. Then as they draw near to the Children of Israel, the Israelites get scared and they begin to exhibit symptoms that need to be cured by the silent treatment. The first symptom that they exhibit is Words that Project Fear.

SYMPTOM #1: WORDS THAT PROJECT FEAR

We hear them say things like "didn't we tell you that we would rather be slaves to the Egyptians than die in the wilderness." Words that project fear always tend to limit options to two equally bad options. Words that project fear create worry, because they show

---

[1] Matthew 11:28,29

solution rather than shifting the blame of the problem. That was somebody's word right there.

Words are not only incorrectly pointed when we or God is the culprit. We must also make sure that we be aware of when this symptom flares up from attacks by the enemy's camp. There would have been no reason for the Children of Israel to be upset about the Egyptian army. The army was really not their problem. Their real problem was Pharaoh whose heart had been hardened. When the lady you don't like at work upsets you, or that church member who is hard to deal with mistreats you, or that mean officer writes you a ticket when you were getting ready to move your car. You've got to realize that you cannot point your words at them, because they are not the problem. There are two issues at play here. The first is that Pharaoh is controlling them. Paul said it like this, "for we wrestle not against flesh and blood, but against principalities, and powers and spiritual wickedness in high places![1]"

The second is that they are acting out of a hardened heart. Friends, we do not know what people go through on a daily basis. That lady at work may upset you because her heart is hardened because she has to go to her second job when she gets off. That church member may be hard to deal with, because his heart is hardened because his cousin is strung out on drugs. That mean officer may still write you that ticket, because his heart is hardened by the hundreds of people that disrespect his position. Friends, Plato said, "that we should be kind, because everyone is fighting a hard battle." That's why words pointed incorrectly is a symptom of needing the silent treatment.

---

[1] Ephesians 6:12

SYMPTOM #3: WORDS THAT PRAISE DEATH

The last symptom that we see are Words that Praise Death. We see it there in verse 11 when the Children of Israel say, "Is it because there were no gravesites in Egypt that we are going to die in this wilderness?" If you noticed, I substituted gravesites for graves, because the word there in the Greek is less about the grave than it is about the memorial that celebrates the life of the deceased. Please make it plain preacher. Yes, mam, I will. Rather than celebrate the new life, which God had liberated from the throes of Egyptian tyranny, they chose to celebrate death with their words.

Proverbs tells us that "life and death are in the power of the tongue.[1]" Do your words speak life and encouragement to people, or do they bring people down and kill them? Do you speak life or death? Somebody said that sticks and stones may break my bones but words will never hurt me. I don't know who said it, but whoever it was that said it is quite mistaken. Because I know that some of the most painful things that I have ever experienced are words. There are some people out there who are still healing from words of death that a loved one or parent or teacher said to you. Some of us are still controlled by those words of death spoken by elementary school children on the playground. Some of us are still running from words of death that make us feel inferior and second-class.

Then more unfortunately some of us produce those words that celebrate death. Those of us who don't need to worry about having haters, because we are the haters. Those of us who never have anything positive to say. Those who when someone tells us good news we find a way to poke a hole in their balloon and rain on their

---

[1] Proverbs 18:21

parade. Perhaps there is no one in here like that, but for the people in here that are like me and know that sometimes my words are harmful, my statements are rash, and my tone is mean. I need for you to say, "Lord, I need a silent treatment."

Fortunately for us, the prescription is right in verse 13. Though it looks like three phrases. In the Greek it is only three imperative verbs. Moses tells the Children of Israel the prescription for your silent treatment. Take courage, stand, and see the salvation of the Lord.

PRESCRIPTION #1: USE WORDS THAT PRAISE LIFE

When Moses tells them to "take courage" it is synonymous to "fear not," because they have to move from a place of great to fear to a place of courage. The only way that they can do this is by turning their backs on words that praise death and turn to words that praise life. You can't speak words of death and get life. You can't consistently feed death through headphones and garbage reality tv and expect life. Sometimes you need to give the silent treatment to Weezy, 2 Chains, and Marvin Gaye, and get the life producing Word of God on the inside of you. I can't go a morning without speaking life. Every morning I take 30 minutes to an hour to speak life over my day and life. Someone may say that they cannot afford to do that, but I've learned that I cannot afford to not do it. Because sometimes stress meets me in the morning, worry prepares breakfast, disappointment irons my clothes, and sadness drives me to work. For a month or so ago, I would wake up and run through my problems and what I needed to do for the day and I was tired before I got out of the bed! But then I started speaking life in the morning and said that "this is the day that the Lord has made, and I will rejoice and be glad in it.[1]"

My perspective changed because when I said, "This is the day" I noticed that the verse used both a demonstrative and definite pronoun to explain that this day is the one that I will rejoice and be glad in. I don't have the privilege of giving God a raincheck, I don't have the prerogative to get credit for yesterday, but this is the day.

Then the verse says "that the Lord has made," so even if things seem random, out of place, unforeseen, and disastrous, the good news is that the Lord made it and everything that God made is good and very good! I know the plans I have for you, declares the Lord, plans for good and not for evil plans to prosper you and to give you and expected end.[2] Then the verse says, "I will rejoice" that is a promise of future action. I don't know what the day holds, but I'm going to rejoice. Though I'm not sure what the answer is going to be, I've already made a commitment to rejoice. Even if death, accidents, or sickness happen today, I have decided and made up in my mind that I will rejoice! "Bless the Lord oh my soul and all that is within me bless his name![3]"

Then the verse declares, "and be glad in it." This originally to me sounded redundant but when I noted that "rejoice" is an action verb, opposed to "be glad" which is a state of being, I noted the difference. Therefore, I have no choice in how I feel. I can't speak death, because I am glad. I cannot be shaken by the day because my name is glad. I refuse to allow my emotions to affect who I have declared myself to be, and I will be glad in this day.

And in this day, I'm not going to praise death with my words, but I am going to praise life. In this day, I'm not going to speak life

---

[1] Psalms 118:24
[2] Jeremiah 29:11
[3] Psalms 103:1

only upon myself, but I am going to speak life to my family, my friends, my associates, and even my enemies. In this day, I refuse to complain about the problems of my situation, but I will celebrate the potential of my circumstances.

So I encourage you to get some verses to enlist in your words that praise life. Verses like "I'm the head and not the tail, above and not beneath, the lender and not the borrower, I'm blessed in the city, blessed in the field, blessed when I come and blessed when I go. Though the enemy comes at me in one way he shall depart in seven.[1]" This is the heritage of Lord that no weapon formed against me shall prosper and every tongue that rises up against me in judgement shall be condemned.[2] Get some verses like "Greater is he that is in me than he is that in the world.[3]" We are more than conquerors through him that loves us. Verses like if God be for me, he is more than the whole world against me.[4] Verses like the Lord is my shepherd, I shall not want![5] Speak life over your family, speak life over you church, speak life over everyone you come into contact with! Let the weak say that I am strong, and let the poor say that I am rich![6] Speak words that celebrate life!

PRESCRIPTION # 2: STAND!

The first prescription is to give the silent treatment to words that praise death and to speak words that praise life. The second prescription comes from Moses' second command "Stand." To fulfill this order we have to give the silent treatment to words that point

---

[1] Deuteronomy 28
[2] Isaiah 54:17,18
[3] I John 4:4
[4] Romans 8:31
[5] Psalms 23:1
[6] Joel 3:10

incorrectly. We saw earlier that words that point incorrectly focus on people and circumstances. The way that we give the silent treatment to those words is by standing. Sometimes you don't have a Scripture or positive statement to give back to someone, so all God asks you to do is to stand.

Frequently, this is the hardest thing for us to do, because we want to be active, we want to be making things happen, but all that God is asking for us to do is to stand. When trouble comes and you feel like cussing somebody out or when you feel like blaming your spouse for why you didn't get the promotion, or you feel like blaming others for your mistakes, take you a little break. Take a few moments, get yourself together, and then stand. Though you feel the heat of the Egyptians exhaling on the back of your neck, stand.

Don't give up, don't give in. They just wanted to see you pushed to the limit. The enemy just wanted to see you blow your fuse and lose your composure. You just have to stand. When you hear news of mass killings and sexual abuse, that's not the time for you to speak words of death and it's not the time for you to blame society or the world. That's the time for you to stand in prayer and say, "I could point this in the direction of the government, but they would only argue about a solution, I could point this in the direction of my friends, but when I went to them for consolation, I found them complaining too.[1] "So God, 'I will lift up mine eyes unto the hills from whence cometh my help'[2] and I know my help comes from you, so I will stand here until your help comes."

---

[1] The Lord Will Make a Way Somehow. By Thomas Dorsey. Online location: http://www.lyricsday.com/The_Hymn-The_Lord_Will_Make_A_Way_Somehow_Lyrics-lyrics-37034908.html
[2] Psalms 121:1

Sometimes you need somebody to stand with you. You don't have to tell them what you need, why you need them to stand, but you should ask somebody, "Will you stand with me?"

Why is it so important that you stand and point your words correctly? It's because the battle is not even about you. The reason why it seems like things are breaking down in your life is not about you. The reason why it seems that nothing is coming together right now is not about you. The reason that it seems like troubles keep coming on every hand is not about you. Ask your neighbor, what then is it about or is he going to have to tell us? Well, if y'all two don't know then let me come to your pew and explain. The reason why things are going the way that they are is so that God can get the glory! God tells Moses that the reason that he's doing all of this is so that He can get glory amongst all of the Egyptians and so that they will know that He is the Lord!

God wants to get the glory. The reason why he wants you to stand and not try to fight back with your words, is because God wants to order the combo. He wants to bring you out and he wants to get all of the glory. He wants to deliver you and get a side of your enemies giving him the praise. He wants to rescue you with a side people wondering how you made. He wants to save you with a side of a smile on your face. So, you just have to stand.

If you talk when you have been called to stand it is similar to when you are on a phone and the call drops and you both keep trying to call each other back, but both phones keep going to voice mail. So the key is that one of you stand and let the other call and then you get through. You missed it. So, God is similarly asking for you to put down your phone and let him call you. But when you are waiting for that special someone to call back it seems like its taking forever, perhaps they forgot, perhaps they won't call back, perhaps they are waiting on me to call them. That's not the case with God, He just wants you to stand in a posture of prayer and wait for Him to give you marching orders across the Red Sea, because "they that wait upon the Lord shall renew their strength and they will mount up with wings like eagles. They will run and not be weary, they shall walk and not faint![1]" Stand!

PRESCRIPTION #3: SEE THE SALVATION OF THE LORD

The last prescription that we find in the text is to "See the salvation of the Lord." This directly corresponds with the symptom of words that project fear. We have to give the silent treatment to words that project fear and see the salvation of the Lord.

We saw earlier that fear limits to two unpleasant options, but when one sees the salvation of the Lord, they see an option that fear wanted to hinder them from seeing. What's interesting about the passage is that it reads differently than I thought it read. I thought it read, fear not, stand, and then you will see the salvation of the Lord. That's not what it says. "See" is also an imperative, so what Moses is commanding them to do is to see something that is not there--to see God doing something fresh and amazing. **To receive the incredible you have to believe the impossible.** Moses is telling them to get God out of the little box that they have confined Him in and imagine Him doing something that the world has never seen. When you replace words that project fear with words that project faith you will be able to see that fear only means finding excuses against relief. Fear only means Finding Excuses Against Relief. If you are fearful or worried, you have just not chosen to see God doing the impossible. It's all about focus. If they shifted their focus, they could have seen

---

[1] Isaiah 40:31

the salvation of the Lord in the fact that they were out of Egypt. But fear made them concerned and gave them an excuse against that relief. Friends, if you are concerned about sickness, you need to see the salvation of the Lord in your body. If you are concerned about your finances, you need to see the salvation of the Lord in your bank account. If you are serious about starting that company, you need to see the salvation of the Lord in that property. You've got to see it.

What definitely helps us to see the salvation of the Lord and overcome anxiety is by talking with him. When fear grips us and tells us that there are only two options, a little time with God will show us that he can make a way out of no way. When we feel like our backs up against the wall, rather than going for a smoke we can talk with God and see him blowing the east wind to deliver us!

THE OUTCOME

Now as I close, I am sure that you want to know what is the outcome of using the silent treatment. The answer is right there in the text. The answer is exciting and amazing. It's right there in verse 14. "The Lord will fight for you!" The word for "fight" there carries connotations of war. So, rather than just seeing it as quick one battle thing, the result of using the silent treatment is that God will fight the war for you. You thought that you were taking courage just for the moment, you thought that you were just standing for that one issue, you thought that you were seeing the salvation of the Lord in getting you across the Red Sea. But God is going to do exceedingly and abundantly above all that you can ask or think[1] and all you have to do is keep silent and let God be God. When you think the battle is over, He will still be fighting, when you make it safely across, He will still

---

[1] Ephesians 3:20

be fighting, when enemy thinks that they can use the pathway that God gave you, He will still be fighting. All you have to do is keep silent and hold your tongue.

Be not dismayed whatever betide,

God will take care of you,

beneath his wings of love abide.

God will take care of you.[1]

The silent treatment was the strategy that Jesus used as they marched him from judgment hall to judgment hall. The old saints would say that he never said a mumbling word.

When Peter tried to confront Him with words that praised death, Jesus gave Him the silent treatment, and spoke life over Peter and said "Even though Satan wants to sift you like wheat when you have been restored you will strengthen your brothers."

In the Garden of Gethsemane, when words pointed incorrectly came into His mind, He gave those words the silent treatment and said "let not my will, but Thine be done!"

As they beat Him, He was silent.

As they lied on Him, He was silent.

As they sold His clothes, He was silent.

When they hung Him on the cross, He was silent.

Then when He hung on the cross between two thieves, the one on the left said if you are really the Son of God then you will get us down. And the one on the right said, "This is a righteous man, so Lord remember me when you enter into your kingdom."

---

[1] God Will Take Care of You. By Civilla Martin. Online location: http://www.cyberhymnal.org/htm/g/w/gwiltake.htm

Jesus responded, He gave the one on the left the silent treatment and he looked at the one on the right, and said "This day will you be with me in paradise!"

Then because Jesus was silent, God fought for him and early on Sunday morning. Before the dew fell on the grass, before the rooster crowed, before the fox left its hole and the bird left its nest.

God braved down through the fiery pits of hell and picked up his Son.

That's where Paul picks up and speaks for Jesus and says, "O death where is thy sting and O grave where is thy victory!"

Does anybody mind being like Paul this morning, and say because he was silent for me, I will speak for him. Because he was quiet for me, I will be loud for him. Because he didn't say a curse word all the time He died, I will bless Him at all times and his praise shall continually be in my mouth.[1]

CALL TO RESPOND

There are some people in here who have some bad habits and enemies that are chasing you, but God is calling you to give them the silent treatment. So close your eyes, and see that problem being drowned in the Red Sea, that issue being drowned, and here is what God says "you will not see them anymore." You're not going back to that job the same anymore, you're not going back to that school the same anymore. This time you are going to use the silent treatment and let God fight for you.

Perhaps He's not fighting for you at all and you want to get Him on your side, you can get saved and get the whole power of God working for you. Perhaps you feel beaten down and broken and you

---

[1] Psalms 34:1

don't know how you are going to stand, you can come too. Or perhaps you want to agree with Moses and say I don't want to see that Egyptian, job-loss, problem, or sin again, and today I want you to agree with me as we watch it drown and use the silent treatment from now on.

4 LOOK AND LIVE

Numbers 21:4b-9 NRSV

but the people became impatient on the way. The people spoke against God and against Moses, "Why have you brought us up out of Egypt to die in the wilderness? For there is no food and no water, and we detest this miserable food." Then the LORD sent poisonous serpents among the people, and they bit the people, so that many Israelites died. The people came to Moses and said, "We have sinned by speaking against the LORD and against you; pray to the LORD to take away the serpents from us." So Moses prayed for the people. And the LORD said to Moses, "Make a poisonous serpent, and set it on a pole; and everyone who is bitten shall look at it and live." So Moses made a serpent of bronze, and put it upon a pole; and whenever a serpent bit someone, that person would look at the serpent of bronze and live.

John 3:13-17 NRSV

No one has ascended into heaven except the one who descended from heaven, the Son of Man. And just as Moses lifted up the serpent in the wilderness, so must the Son of Man be lifted up, that whoever believes in him may have eternal life. "For God so loved the world that he gave his only Son, so that everyone who believes in him may not perish but may have eternal life. "Indeed, God did not send the Son into the world to condemn the world, but in order that the world might be saved through him.

In Greek mythology, there is a story of someone who you may find familiar, Narcissus. As you know, this character was handsome, beautiful, a pretty boy if you will. He was prophesied to that he would live to be an old age if he would never look at himself. However, after he kept getting chose and after countless lovers attempted to gain his affection and he refused to return it, he was led to a pool where he saw his reflection. There he fell in love with *himself.* There he was stuck looking at *himself.* There he could not leave, because he could not be without *himself.* There he died with *himself.* That's such a preposterous story, that's such an unbelievable narrative that his name has been associated with any similar vanity or narcissism. However, I must inform you that Narcissus is not the only individual, mythical or actual, that has died as a result of looking at *herself.*

It is quite fascinating that the letter "I" is at the center of the word "die." For to me, it shows an ideal indicator of the seriousness of taking our eyes off of God's path, purpose, and power for our lives and shifting our focus to I. When our lives become centered only on our impatience, our insecurities, and our impotencies we literally begin to die. Come here Adam. When did you die, get kicked out of the garden, and lose fellowship with God? Adam would respond, "Well, Jeremy, when I saw something good for my eyes and didn't want to wait for God to give it to me (lust of the eyes[1]). Then when I felt like the serpent was offering me something that God had not already given me several times over (lust of the flesh). And then, Jeremy, as if that's not enough, when I felt like I didn't have any power, because I was not as wise as God, even though He had made me in His image and his very breath was in my nostrils. The day I

---

[1] 1 John 2:16

stopped looking at God and looking at myself I died." I feel like Adam would admonish everyone in here today to "Look and Live."

However, that is not an easy lesson, for in our text we see that the Children of Israel did not get it either. They have their own run in with serpents. And this time it's not the tenacious tongues of the sneaky snakes that tempt the tribes. Rather it is their ferocious fangs that pack poisonous bites. Originally, upon reading this text I was perplexed by the thought that the Lord (*Kurios*) would send poisonous serpents among these people to kill them. Then the Holy Ghost showed me that God did not send the snakes just to be malicious, but rather He sent them to physically show the corrosion that had already happened spiritually, mentally, and emotionally. They had died long before the snakes started biting. They had died when they shifted their gaze from the path, purpose, and power of God to their tired, timid, and tacky selves. This fatal refocusing can be seen clearly in three different ways via our text.

SERPENT OF IMPATIENCE

First, *but the people became impatient on the way.* The Israelites got to the point where they stopped caring where they were going and just wanted to get there. Have you been there? A place where you feel like you've been going, going, going and going around in circles and you don't even care where you're going anymore, you just want to GET SOMEWHERE so you can stop going?! You want to graduate so you can stop going to school. You want a new career, so you can stop going to that old job. You want a new car, so you can stop going to the shop to get yours fixed. Friends, you may not like this, but we must learn to be content. Why? Because **impatience robs you of your journey, and doesn't get you to your goal any quicker.** Let me say that again. Impatience robs you of your journey, and doesn't get you to your goal any quicker. This understanding will help you to make friends in unfamiliar places, it will help you to turn waiting time into preparation time, and it will help you transform lemons into lemonade. Or better yet, as my little cousin says it will allow you to take the seeds out of the bitter lemon and then sow them so that they become blossoming, profitable lemon trees.

This brings new meaning to one of our favorite verses, for it is not just in times of stress or challenge, but it is also in times that require patience that I can draw from the wells of Philippians 4:13 and declare that "I can do all things through Christ who strengthens me!" Knowing that even though I want this to hurry up and be over, knowing that I want the end to come. I can make it, because I only have to make it one day at a time. Time machines only exist in movies and sci-fi, but in our lives we can only get to the degree, the diploma, the development one day at a time. Sometimes those days seem unbearable and intolerable especially when we see them piling up into weeks of worry, months of misery, quarters of questions, years of yearning, and futures of fear. But as Abraham Lincoln said, "the best thing about the future for us is that it comes only one day at time." That's why the Scriptures talk about "Today" being the day of salvation, because this is the only day you have ever had and will ever have, so make today count. Don't use it to look at how long it will take for you to recuperate from your past. Don't use it to look at how long it will take you to get to your promised future. Those ways can lead to poisonous serpent bites of impatience that lead to death. But look and live by heeding Paul's advice to the Galatians to not "grow weary in well doing, knowing that in due season you will reap if you don't give up." Look and live, listening to the Psalmist who declared, "wait on the Lord and be of good courage and he will strengthen your heart." Look and live, understanding Isaiah's words prophesying that "they that wait upon the Lord shall renew their strength and shall mount up with wings like eagles. They shall run and not be weary and they shall walk and not faint." Look and Live!

SERPENT OF INSECURITY

Second, *"for there is no food and no water, and we detest this miserable food."* Perceived lack breeds insecurity. You will never find anyone insecure who does not *perceive* that they lack something. This week I read an article in Yahoo news about Kim Kardashian. For those of you who do not know her she is famous for... ...... being famous. Many would claim that she is extremely attractive and she consistently ranks in magazines and polls as one of the most attractive women in the world. However, she wrestles sometimes with feeling attractive, because of imperfections that she sees. However, she gives a piece of advice that the Israelites could have you used. She says, "you have to look in the mirror and like what you see!"

In our passage the Israelites could only see their lack. They could only see what they didn't have. They could only see the food that they lacked. And with the food they had, they could only see the food that they didn't want. This lack led to a death of their self-confidence and self-worth. They did not need any bullying because they were beating up on themselves. They were looking at themselves and the serpent of insecurity bit them in their blemishes, licked them in their lack, and slid in their self-pity.

So, they were ashamed of the apparent flaws that they tried to cover up with makeup. They were ashamed of being overweight in comparison to those on the stage of pop music. They were ashamed of not being able to afford the name brands. So, they lashed out on those closest to them, Moses their leader and they even lashed out on God. This was not because they were bad. But it was because they were going through changes. Middle school hormonal changes have you mad and you don't know why. Then you're so upset that you upset everybody else in the house. Insecurities. High school social changes force you to decide what you stand for when popularity, peer pressure, and pals are on the line. Insecurities. College life changes leave you feeling unequipped to take on the world by yourself. Insecurities. Whether you want to admit it or not there is some situation that makes you feel insecure. It seems that the people with the most insecurities like to talk about what they see others lacking ie bullies. Freud calls it "projecting." For, the flaws we often call out in others are either those, which we have ourselves, or they are the ones that we can use to divert others from seeing our real flaws. That brings new meaning to what they taught us when they said that "I am rubber and you are glue. Whatever you say, bounces off of me and sticks right back on to you." Friends, we all have flaws and we cannot afford to call out each other for cheap laughs or to make ourselves feel better.

From finances to relationships to health, there are some aspects in your life that make you feel like you are lacking resources. The truth is, you probably are lacking resources, but I have come to tell you that even though your resources may be limited your Source never runs out! (Tweet that) When your financial resources are low, He promised that He would "supply all of your needs according to his riches in glory.[1]" When your health resources are low, we know that "with His stripes we are healed.[2]" When your peace is low, he

---

[1] Philippians 4:19
[2] Isaiah 53:5

will give you "peace that passes all understanding.[1]" To cover all of the bases, when your whatever is low, (yeah I said your "whatever") He said, "ask, and it shall be given, knock and the door shall be open unto you, seek and you shall find![2]"

Why is he willing to do all of this you may ask? Why is he willing to assist someone so helpless, wretched, and unworthy as me? It is because He does not care about that. That's what justification is. He sees that you are messed up, disgusted, trifling, and disagreeable, but God does not care about that. He loves you, because you believe He loves you. As a matter of fact, He loved you even before you believed. That's why He did not even spare His only Son for you! Don't let the serpent of insecurity bite you about your looks because you are beautifully and wonderfully made.[3] Don't let the serpent of insecurity bite you about your status, because you're an heir of God and join heir with Jesus Christ.[4] And don't let the serpent of insecurity bite you about your past and your vices, because there is therefore now no condemnation to those who are in Christ![5] Look and Live.

SERPENT OF IMPOTENCE

Finally, *Why have you brought us up out of Egypt to die in the wilderness?* These Israelites were dreadful. They were full of dread. Those with elementary knowledge of chemistry know that you can't be full of two things at the same time. Even in spite of what Future[6]

---

[1] Philippians 4:7
[2] Matthew 7:7
[3] Psalms 139:14
[4] Romans 8:17
[5] Romans 8:1
[6] Popular rapper

said. One can't be full of faith and full of fear. One cannot be full of hate and full of love. They can't be full of dread and full of the power of God. Friends, you can't be full of anything else if you are full of God. Because they were full of dread they could not experience the power of God operating in their lives. They could not even bear witness to the power of God that had operated previously in their lives because they were bitten by the serpent of impotence. Here in their impatience and insecurity they also felt impotent. They felt that they couldn't change anything in their lives. They felt like they did not have any power or any agency make things better. It seemed like the only answer was death.

Perhaps, you may have felt that the only way to get out of the situation was giving up, quitting, throwing in the towel, or even death. Friends, don't get so saved on me that you think that Christians don't contemplate suicide. There are those times when our backs are up against the wall and it seems as the waters are rising swiftly that there is no other course of action. You feel that you need to get out or the enemy is going to take you out!

When you look back to Egypt, you give the serpent of impotence an opportunity to bite. For it's then that you feel as if you do not deserve to possess the promises that God planned for you. You feel that you are a runaway slave rather than a released freeperson. You feel that this is too good to be true, food raining down from heaven, clothes not getting old, no one is getting sick around you. You feel that something bad is going to have to happen, because you belong in Egypt. Where you have no power, where you allow the systems of this world to make decisions for you, and where you do as you are told without thought or questions. You have no rights. You have no power. You are impotent.

LOOK AT POWER, PURPOSE & PATIENCE

Your Power

This thinking is actually not completely wrong. It is partially incorrect, and partially correct. Let's address the incorrect portion first. You do have power to transform your miserable circling-around-wilderness story into a journey to the promise land narrative. You are no longer a slave in Egypt, but you are now a citizen of the Kingdom of God and you can exercise the rights and privileges thereof. God has not called you to darkness and to death, but rather He has "called you from the darkness into the marvelous light that you may show forth his praises for you are a royal priesthood, a holy nation, a chosen generation![1]" You are not in the wilderness to complain about God, but you are here to call to God. Remember, that's why they left Egypt, to worship God in the wilderness.

Let me take this brief caveat, the only people that complain are people that have no power or influence. The next time you complain notice why. It is because you felt powerless, and you wanted to tell somebody about it, so that they could throw a pity party with you. I am guilty of complaining a lot myself. So, the Lord asked me a question, if you are going to talk about it, why not talk to somebody who can do something about it. Rather than going to your "friends for consolation and you find them complaining too![2]"

You see the Israelites thought that they were responsible for the power, so when they felt like they didn't have it, they began to complain. However, if they actually understood their power they

[1] 2 Peter 2:9
[2] The Lord Will Make a Way Somehow. By Thomas Dorsey. Online location: http://www.lyricsday.com/The_Hymn-The_Lord_Will_Make_A_Way_Somehow_Lyrics-lyrics-37034908.html

would have done what they did in verse 7 and they would have called out to God through Moses. For, He is the only one that can do something about their situation. Only as co-workers with God could they expect for their situation to change. You see their power was not in their complaining it was in their calling. It was not in their hollering it was in their humbling. Yes, their power was in them humbling themselves to Almighty God. Then they could realize that meekness is not weakness, it's power under control. If they could humble themselves, then God could do amazing things through them. We can see this in President Obama's 2012 nomination acceptance speech. He did not pounce all over his opponents and complain about their lies and misrepresentations. Rather, he told what he had accomplished and wanted to accomplish and humbled himself before the American people. He had power under control.

Complaining and looking toward Egypt never made manna fall from the sky or a Red Sea split. But what did make manna fall from the sky was looking up to heaven and saying, "Lord if you don't do it won't get done." That's when God uses human hands and tools to transform the course of human history. Will you be humble enough to let the power of God work through you to live a life that's pleasing to Him? Will you be humble enough to let the power of God use you to go to the voting both even though Alabama is a red state? Will you be humble enough to be like Job and declare "though he slay me, yet will I trust him." Will you be humble enough to declare like the Psalmist, "I will lift up mine eyes unto the hills from whence cometh my help, and my help comes from the Lord!" I will. Look and Live.

His Power

We just saw that in thinking that we have no power we are wrong in some ways. However, in other ways, it is actually correct. For, often we find ourselves like these Children of Israel having allowed our lives to be bitten by serpents of impatience, insecurity, and impotence. These are times when we have no control, no power, no authority. Why? We have taken on something way bigger than ourselves. We have challenged God and his throne, by believing that we can bring better order to our lives than He can, and this alienates us from His power. We have attempted to tackle thematic injustices of evil, racism, sexism, and poverty on our own but our personal efforts seem futile. We have tried to bring down negative and destructive thoughts, but our efforts always come short. We have tried to do unto others as we would have them do unto us, but our temper, attitude, and selfishness get in the way. We are impotent like the Children of Israel, lame in our wilderness without agency and authority to combat our sin.

Friends, there is but One Solution who can stop the never ending chain of events that have evolved from our hurtful words, mindless actions, egregious greed, unbecoming hate, unbelievable meanness, terrible dishonesty, and destructive ways. We have looked to ourselves and our very nature has been bitten by the serpent of sin, so its poison runs through every bit over bodies. So, "who shall deliver us from the body of this flesh?!"[1]

There is but One Solution that can stop the venom of sin before we become spiritual corpses to never rise again. Look, look, look, look there under the altar is a lamb that looks like it has been

---

[1] Romans 7:24

slain.[1] Behold the Lamb of God that takes away the sins of the world.[2] Look there at Moses as he typifies the solution. There he takes a precious metal and forms it into the shape of the object that was afflicting them and lifts it up. Then those who look are healed.

There friends is the solution to our impotence. Look and see God taking His precious Word and wrapping it in the stench and ugliness of broken promises, unfulfilled dreams, and unrealized potential. Look at God taking His precious Son and forming Him into the shape of humans, so that humans can be shaped in the form of Him. Then look at God hoisting him on a tree on a hill, and lifting Him so that everyone can see.

How to reach the masses men of every birth
For an answer Jesus gave the key
He said, "And I, if I be lifted up from the earth
Will draw all men unto me.[3]"

Interestingly, in the Numbers passage, we do not see a command for everyone to look at the serpent. However, they without prompting and prodding look toward this object that is both appalling and appealing. It is both menacing and magnetizing. For there they saw the emblem of the plague that was afflicting them. There they saw the enemy that took away their loved ones. There they saw the sickness that was in their bodies. Is this not the cross?

There we see grievous punishment for our errors, mistakes, and issues. We are repulsed by the cruelty of humanity of which we all share a part. We are devastated by our impatience as He endured the

---

[1] Revelation 5:6
[2] John 1:29
[3] Lift Him Up. By Johnson Oatman, Jr. Online location: http://www.cyberhymnal.org/htm/l/i/f/lifthimu.htm

cross and despised the shame. We are appalled by our insecurities as He hangs naked atop Calvary. We marvel at our impotence as He cries for someone else to give him something to drink, "surely he hath borne our grief and carried our sorrows.[1]"

However, not only did this image bring death, but it brought life. Look beyond the frustration and impatience that flow from the rivers of His tears, and see the rolled away stone of the resurrection that shows that God has not forgotten us in our perseverance. Look and see that God is not slack concerning His promises.[2] Look and see that God is able to do just what he said he would do. He's going to fulfill every promise to you.[3]" Look and see that we have a better cure, because those who had been bitten and did not see the bronze serpent were dead, but in Jesus Christ we see that death does not limit God and He will raise you from the dead. And because He lives, "I can face tomorrow, and life is worth the living just because He lives."

Look at His words from Calvary, words that seem filled with desperation. Look at His words that seem insecure noting that His friends had left Him, the crowd had turned on Him, and it even seemed that God had deserted Him. Look behind the "My God, my God why has though forsaken me.[4]" And see His evening chat with Nicodemus that "For God so loved the world…" Yes, the world that is messed up. Yes, the world that rebels against God. Yes, the world that is imperfect and dysfunctional. Look and see that for this messed up world, God gave His only begotten Son that whosoever believeth in Him should not perish, but have everlasting life.

---

[1] Isaiah 53:4
[2] 2 Peter 3:9
[3] He's Able. By Deittrick Haddon. Online location:
http://www.lyricsmania.com/hes_able_lyrics_deitrick_haddon.html
[4] Matthew 27:46

Look and see that as the cat-of-nine tails and spear pierced his flesh like serpent bites. Look at how they seemed to expose his weakness and impotence. Look, how they actually released the power of God by shedding His blood. For "there is power, power wondrous working power in the blood of the Lamb.[1]" The blood that "reaches to the highest mountain and flows to the lowest valley. The blood that gives me strength from day to day, it will never lose power![2]"

Look at the Power of God in Christ's shed blood!
Look at the Purpose of God in the midst of our frailties!
Look at the Patience of Christ enduring on our behalves!
Look and Live!

---

[1] There Is Power in the Blood. By Lewis E. Jones. Online Location: library.timeless.org/music/there_is_power_in_the_blood/
[2] The Blood Will Never Lose It's Power. By Clay Crosse. Online Location: http://m.metrolyrics.com/the-blood-will-never-lose-its -power-lyrics-crosse.html

5 CAN I HAVE THIS DANCE?

2 Samuel 6: 1-**13-16**

[13]and when those who bore the ark of the LORD had gone six paces, he sacrificed an ox and a fatling. [14]David danced before the LORD with all his might; David was girded with a linen ephod. [15]So David and all the house of Israel brought up the ark of theLORD with shouting, and with the sound of the trumpet.16 As the ark of the LORD came into the city of David, Michal daughter of Saul looked out of the window, and saw King David leaping and dancing before the LORD; and she despised him in her heart.

Mark 6:14-**22-24**-28

[22]When his daughter Herodias came in and danced, she pleased Herod and his guests; and the king said to the girl, 'Ask me for whatever you wish, and I will give it.' [23]And he solemnly swore to her, 'Whatever you ask me, I will give you, even half of my kingdom.'[24]She went out and said to her mother, 'What should I ask for?' She replied, 'The head of John the baptizer.'

Go with me to an event where there is dancing. Whether it's a party, a wedding reception, or any number of places where there is a dance floor. And please don't act like you have not been anywhere like that. Well, if you haven't I have. Imagine a lonely attractive young lady, standing alone on the dance floor. Perhaps dancing a little, but you know that she really wants to dance with somebody. So, a young man, handsome, about 6 feet tall, that's dressed like a pretty boy, walks up to her and asks her to dance. Or let me be transparent, he takes her and starts dancing. There are questions that run through her mind as she considers dancing with the guy. Who is he? Who's watching? What song is on? Similarly, with questions like those we can see the stark contrast between the dancers and their response to God's question "Can I Have This Dance?"

WHO'S WATCHING?

In both passages, "Who's watching?" is an important question. We know that it's important, because from our context a lot of the places where we dance are dark, because we don't want anybody watching. That's not what I'm here to discuss tonight; however, in our passages we can see a question of "who's watching?"

Let me give you the quick fly over view of both stories to show you the audience. In II Samuel 6 we see King David getting the Ark of the Covenant from Obed-edom's house after a failed attempt to bring it to Jerusalem. After seeing the blessing of the Lord on Obed-edom's family, he decides to go and get the Ark and bring it home with the correct precautions. As he walks in the parade in front of all of Israel with the equivalent of a marching band behind him, he dances wildly in praises to God. He dances so that his wife, Michal, gets ashamed and calls him out on it and subtweets him saying "Somebody made a fool of himself today." His dance was for God.

Now let's fast forward several hundred years to the birthday party of Herod Antipas, it may have been a white party, but what we do know is that all of the officials of Judaea were there to celebrate and pop bottles with Herod. He had John the Baptist in jail, because John had told him that he shouldn't be married to his brother's wife. Herod's wife didn't like the fact that John had said that, so she told Herod to lock him up. Mark conveys that Herod did not really want to do that, because he knew that John was a righteous and holy man. So in this party comes his daughter (and perhaps also his niece.) whom Josephus identifies as Salome. And she dances so that he offers her up to half of his kingdom. She goes to ask her mother what to get and Herodias tells her to get the head of John the Baptist on a silver platter. Her dance was for Herod.

Now we see the audiences of the two dancers. There were two different groups watching so there were two very different dances. We understand the role of the audience with dancing, because we know the challenge of pulling a girl away from a group of "saddity" friends and if she had been on her own she would have danced with you without any hesitation. Perhaps, I need to put it this way. There are some dances that you would do on Saturday night that you would not do Sunday morning, because of the audience.

Dance for Herod: John's Head on a Silver Platter

So, in Mark's telling of Herod's birthday party, we see the audience of distinguished leaders, so Herod presents himself as larger than life to keep up with the lords, captains, and Joneses of his time. So upon seeing the dance, he offers up to half of his kingdom, something that he could not really afford. But the reason that he offered it is because no one else around him could even offer an award that size. He wanted to show his power over resources, his position over people, and his prestige over his guest and he went overboard. That is so similar to how we spend money that we don't have on things that we can't afford to impress people that we don't know and don't like. This dance for Herod represents acting in a way to get the approval of others. Friends, dancing for the approval of the audience will always leave you disappointed. Bill Cosby said it like this, "I don't know the key to success, but the key to failure is trying to please everybody."

Someone's not going to like the way you look, how you act, or how you perform. And in an attempt to try to make people accept you and appreciate you, you will give up your values and what's really important to you. That's John's head on a silver platter. When we don't follow the advice of those who care about us, and attempt to silence them in a prison of apathy—that's John's head on a platter. When we know what's right to do, but we choose to conform to be like everyone else we're putting John's head on a platter. When we give up our own dreams, to pursue someone else's because it's the path of least resistance, we're putting John's head on a platter. Why is this? Because we were made to be individually and uniquely us. We are beautifully and wonderfully made to make good independent choices.

However, when we join in the mob mentality we can get John's head cut off or even worse. Jesus gets crucified when we don't exercise our individuality. Bishop Joseph Johnson of our Church said that "whenever we choose the difficult right over the easy wrong, we gain our lives." You don't have to try to be like anybody else or want what they have. Emerson says that "Envy is ignorance, Imitation is

Suicide." Mama said it like this "What God has for me is for me!" If God wanted me differently he would have made me that way, and if there are two of me then one of us is useless!

Dance for God

Here we see why David's dance for God is so powerful, because he is not concerned about what the crowd has to say about him. Sure, he hears people saying that it doesn't take all of that. Sure, he hears people say that the king shouldn't do that. Sure, he hears that CME's don't do that. That does not bother him, because he knows who he is and who God has made him to be. If people think that he looked foolish or not he is still the king. Some say he danced his clothes off, but even if he did, he was still the king. Even if he wanted to be conservative and rock back and forth he was still the king. Why? Because in spite of what the people said, they had no hand in making him king. God had selected him without anybody else's permission or approval. He didn't take it before the General, Annual, District, Quarterly, or Church Conference! No person's input elected David, so no person's input could impeach David. That's why David danced like he did. He didn't have to do someone else's dance, he could just do his own. Similarly, God is calling you to do your own dance. You don't have to crank somebody else or do the Charlie Boy Gang's "Beef It Up.[1]" You can do your own dance. Dream Better Dreams.

Here's what David told his wife Michal who was ashamed at her husband. He said, "I understand that you were raised in the palace, I understand that you always understood that you were a child of the king. But when I look back over my life and how I went from being a

---

[1] Popular dance

shepherd's son to the king of Israel, I've got to dance for God. When I think of all of the times that I should have been killed by ravenous animals, mauled by talkative giants, and murdered by depressing Philistines. I've got to dance for the Lord." Somebody in here can join in with David and say that when I should have failed that class, when I should have been evicted from my house, when I should have gotten a disease, when I should have been dead, when other people said that I was unqualified, not old enough, or too old and God saw fit to use me anyway. How I came from a single parent home, went to a dead end high school, but then graduated from Vanderbilt and now headed to Yale! So, I have to dance for Him, because of who he has made me to be, and he doesn't care if I have two left feet, don't have rhythm, or just don't how to dance So, yes, Lord you can have this dance!"

What's Playing?

Along with the audience and the question of who's watching, there's another important question, "What's playing?" Frequently, the song determines how and if she will dance. Music is indeed important, because it has a unique ability to transcend our minds and capture our emotions. That's why music is instrumental in worship in setting an atmosphere. However, that is not the only place that it is utilized. It is not only used in dancing for God but it was used in dancing for Herod. For, I imagine that there was music at Herod's party, and it wasn't "Oh give thanks to the Lord.[1]" They weren't blasting "Great is thy Faithfulness.[2]" Nor were they playing "I

---

[1] Psalm 136:1

[2] Great is Thy Faithfulness. By Thomas O. Chisholm. 1923. Online Location: www.hymntime.com/tch/htm/g/r/e/greatif

Smile.[1]" The music would have been more along the lines of songs from Made Back Music, Young Money, Jeezy, Future, or Chris Brown.[2]

This music prompted the movements of Herod's daughter to move in ways that provoked a response. Seeing the girl sway to the music made Herod want to act, her body made him want to make it rain, it made him willing to give up half of his kingdom. For a dance! He was willing to give up a majority of what he had for one moment and one dance. His emotions took over and by the time he came to himself from the emotional high he realized that the few moments of pleasure were not worth the lifetime of pain that he would have to endure. (You can connect that one for yourself.) Friends, dancing for Herod is living life and making important decisions based on emotions, based on Basketball Wives, based on artist's lyrics. It is living based on a song.

Who's the DJ?

When the song is good your up, but when the song is bad you sit down. In this regard the DJ controls the entire event, because their mixing controls people's responses. Friends, if we are not careful then Herodias may be on the ones and twos in the DJ booth creating a plan that will destroy you and God's plan for your life. Every time that we allow ourselves to go against our personal code of ethics and dance to the music of hatred, intolerance, self-centeredness, and rebellion, we lose focus on who God has made us to be. You can't be governed just by how you feel. **If you base decisions off of a song, you will be the one that gets played.**

---

[1] I Smile. Kirk Franklin. www.azlyrics.com/kirkfranklin/ismile.html
[2] Popular labels and music artists in 2012

For the song is only temporary, the feelings are only temporary, but the consequences may not be so temporary. Just because the right words are being said, and it seems that he's doing the right things you don't have to dance for Herod. I challenge you every time that you feel like cursing somebody out ask yourself? Am I dancing for Herod or for God? Whenever your cheating boyfriend calls you over again, ask "Am I dancing for Herod or for God?" Whenever you feel like quitting and giving up, ponder, "Am I dancing for Herod or for God?"

The Dance of Triumph

It is easy to discern to whom you are dancing, because dancing for Herod takes opportunity by your flesh and emotional weaknesses, but dancing for God is a shift from focusing on the temporary to the eternal. It captures the true essence of dance, because in the Hebrew Bible, especially in the books of Law and History the word dance is only used to discuss triumphs. Triumphing over the Egyptians, triumphing over Philistines, and triumphing over giants. But in II Samuel 6 what is Daniel triumphing over? The Hittites, the Hivites, the Jebusites and all the others ites have been moved, but what is left? It's there in the text in verse 9. It is humanity's greatest giant, the fear of death. The Bible says that David was afraid, which in many ways is rightly so, because God had just struck down Uzzah, because he had mishandled the ark of the covenant.

The music of praise and hope had turned into a music of bereavement and hopelessness. But then David started to see something going on down at Obed-edom's house. He saw that he was being blessed! It was then that he realized that God did not want to destroy him with death, but that he wanted to bless him with life.

And knowing that God had given him triumph over this fear, it was time to pull out the ephod and get to dancing. Knowing that God has given us the ultimate victory takes power away from those moments that seem like they can overtake us. Knowing that we are more than conquerors[1] gives us control over those urges that try to overwhelm. Knowing that greater is he that is in us[2] gives us the power over our decisions. So then it does not matter what is playing we can still dance because we have the triumph. "Because he lives I can face tomorrow, because he lives all fear is gone, because I know who holds the future and life is worth the living just because he lives.[3]"

David the Songwriter

David understood this so well that he could dance at any song, and if he couldn't find the right song on his iPod he would write a song. When he was feeling good, he wrote "the Lord is my light and my salvation.[4]" When he felt down and had the blues he wrote "have mercy upon me according to your tender mercies.[5]" When he was out in the field one day he in the country he wrote, "The Lord is my shepherd and I shall not want.[6]" And even if he did not have a particular song, he was so confident in his victory that he declared, "I will bless the Lord at all times and his praise shall continually be in my mouth.[7]" God is asking for some people like that to dance with him who will dance, not based on their feelings, or if they like the

[1] Romans 8:37

[2] I John 4:4

[3] Because He Lives. Bill and Gloria Gaither. Online Location: www.hymnlyrics.org/mostpopularhymns/because_he_lives.htm

[4] Psalms 27:1

[5] 5 Psalms 51:1

[6] Psalms 23:1

[7] Psalms 34:1

song, or if their singer is singing, but He is looking for people that will dance at all times. If R&B is playing they will dance. If the blues is playing they will dance. And even if rock and country are playing they will dance, because they understand that they are the head and not the tail above and not beneath, the lender and not the borrow, [1] and they understand that if God is for them who can be against them. [2] So no weapon formed against them shall prosper. [3] Sounds like a good reason to me to dance for God regardless of the music.

WHO'S WATCHING?

Now for the subtle yet most obvious question outside of "who's watching" and "What's playing?" The real question is "who's asking?" In these two passages we see a stark difference between when Herod asks for the dance and when God asks for a dance.

Herod's response to the dance is not participation, it is payment. He looks at the dancer and rather than have a conversation and congratulate her skills, he wants to put a price on the dance and in effect the girl. He asks, "How much?" He turns her into an object, possibly even a sexual one (this is not to be ruled out even though it is Herodias' daughter, because Herod's morals are questionable at best, because he is married to his brother's wife.) Here we see dancing, normally a symbol of triumph and beauty transformed into something ugly. Why? Because the inviter does not see the shared humanity, but rather sees an object that can be used for his own gratification. In this moment, Salome is not his little girl, but she is nothing more than a body, a number, a notch on his belt.

---

[1] Deuteronomy 28

[2] Romans 8:31

[3] Isaiah 54:17

Friends, we can look bad at Herod, but how frequently have we men objectified women to be nothing more than objects of our own satisfaction. For many guys, we have even turned this into a standard of our masculinity, how many female human beings we can turn into objects and get what we want. This is the result of when we view our own humanness as more valuable than others. I can't let the women off the hook either, because you know what you are doing when you give the eye from across the room. When you turn your sexuality into a bargaining chip. When we see each other as only objects we see teenage pregnancy rates increase. When we see each other as objects cases of HIV and AIDs increase in our community. When we see each other as objects we see people with those two issues as unsavable. We cannot look at each other as objects with a price tag that we determine. That friends, is dancing for Herod.

She Got It From Her Momma!

But perhaps, someone is like me and wants to know, where did this girl learn to dance like that? Where did she learn to allow herself to become an object. Was it greater society? Was it BET? Was it reality television? If you look closely in the text, she got it from her "momma." She learned from her mother how to manipulate a man, she learned from her mother that she had to do what she had to do to get what she wanted, she learned from her mother that there is a certain thing to do to get someone's attention. She learned from previous generations that she needed to wear make-up to be beautiful, she learned from her elders that her body needed to be a certain size to be attractive, she learned from her mentors that her hair needed to be longer to be fine. It was her mother who passed down patriarchal ideas of beauty and submission that told her to be less than a person. That is what dancing for Herod will do for you.

I am so glad that when God asks for this dance, he does not turn us into any object for his personal gratification. He does not look at us and see a price tag. He who did not withhold his own Son, but gave Him up for all of us, will he not with him also give us everything else?[1]

"Can I Have This Dance?" ~God

When God asks us to dance, He asks us to dance as a groom dances with his bride. He doesn't care if we are big, small, young, old, weaved, natural, pretty or homely. But He just wants us to dance with Him, and he wants you to know in the words of Missy Elliot nobody's perfect, but you're perfect for me. He is asking, "Can I have this dance regardless of who's watching?" He's asking, "Can I have this dance in spite of how you feel?"

Someone may wonder who is this that is asking for me to dance?

He is the One that choreographed the dolphin's dance.
He is the One that penned the songs that bird's sing.
He is the One that crafted the movements of the gazelle.
He is the One that created the melodies of the deep.
He is the One that directs the symphony of nature.

Someone still may be wondering why I would want to dance with him.

[1]Romans 8:31

Miriam would tell you that, "I will dance with him, because he turned the Red Sea into a dance floor.[1]"

David would tell you that, "I will dance for him, because He asked me to dance, when even my family had counted me out, and he told me that when your mother and father forsake you then I will bear you up.[2]

The paralytic at the Beautiful gate would tell you, "I will dance for him, because I came paralyzed looking for him to put money in my pocket, but instead he putt clapping in my hands, stomping in my feet, a praise on my lips and dancing in my legs. [3]"

Those are some examples in the past, if we fast forward to the future.

John said that he saw the marriage supper of the Lamb where the Church is adorned as His Bride,[4] and I just imagine that at the reception that there is going to be some dancing. I just imagine that sometime during that reception that the Lord is going to walk over, and ask "Can I have this dance?" I don't know how he's going to dance with all of us, but even if it is the wobble, the cupid shuffle, or the electric slide,[5] I will say "Yes." Yes, you can have this dance." Yes, I want to dance with you!

Why? Because "He took the shackles off my feet so I can dance. He exchanged my sackcloth for a garment of praise, and traded out my mourning for dancing. As Whitney said, "I want to dance with somebody who loves me."

So I will dance for him.

---

[1] Exodus 15
[2] Psalms 27:10
[3] Acts 3
[4] Revelation 19, 21
[5] Popular line dances

I'll dance, passed when the DJ turns off the music.

I'll dance passed when the lights come on.

I'll dance passed when the mountains fade away.

I'll dance, passed when the moon turns into blood.

I'll dance, passed when time that has been won't be anymore.

I will dance into eternity with legs that won't get tired.

Lord, I'll go what you want me to do. I'll be who you have made me to be. I'll praise you regardless of how I feel. I'll value people the way you value me. What ever you ask me to do, I'll say "yes." If you can use anybody, you can use me!

BONUS CHAPTER:
I'VE GOT TO GET MY HARVEST

Psalm 126

When the LORD *turned again the captivity of Zion, we were like them that dream.* [2] *Then was our mouth filled with laughter, and our tongue with singing: then said they among the heathen, The* LORD *hath done great things for them.* [3] *The* LORD *hath done great things for us; whereof we are glad.* [4] *Turn again our captivity, O* LORD, *as the streams in the south.* [5] *They that sow in tears shall reap in joy.* [6] *He that goeth forth and weepeth, bearing precious seed, shall doubtless come again with rejoicing, bringing his sheaves with him.*

Let me share a story with you:

There was a man, who they called Crazy Quincy, and he decided that he was going to start farming. So, he bought some land and plowed it. Then, the next day he went outside to see his harvest, and he was disappointed. So, he went over and asked Frank the Farmer why he did not have a harvest.

Frank said with a Southern drawl, "You know the Bible says, 'you reap what you sow.' What'd you sow?"

Quincy, a little embarrassed said, "I didn't sow anything."

Frank said, "Well, that's your first problem, and..."

Before Frank could finish his sentence, Crazy Quincy had gone to the store and hastily picked up some seeds. He took them back to his farm and planted them. When he woke up the next morning to look at his harvest, he saw nothing. Disappointed again, he went and talked with Frank the Farmer.

Crazy Quincy said, "Now Frank, man, I planted some seeds and I still don't have a harvest."

Frank responded wisely saying, "Well, the Bible says that there will be 'seedtime and harvest.' I reckon that there is reason that the word "time" is between seed and harvest. So, you have to prepare, water, and fertilize the seeds. Now what kind of..."

Before Frank could finish, Crazy Quincy had started his farming plan of watering, fertilizing and preparing for his harvest. He worked hard and diligently for weeks and he started seeing sprouts and growth. Then one day he woke up disappointed again. He pulled out a knife and cut some of his produce and he took it over to Frank the Farmer's house.

Crazy Quincy held up the produce in his hand and says, "Frank, what is this?"

Frank examined it and then remarked, "It looks like a stalk of corn to me."

Quincy responded, "That's not what I wanted! I wanted watermelon."

That statement even shocked Frank, and after he got himself together he asked, "Well, what kind of seed did you plant?"

Quincy retorted angrily, "I don't know! Why? Was I supposed to pay attention to that?"

Lessons from Crazy Quincy

Friends, this story may seem comical. However, how frequently do we look like Crazy Quincy? How many times do we expect for God to give us a harvest without even planting anything? How many times do we want God to give us a harvest without preparing for one? How many times do we get a harvest and don't get what we want, because we didn't pay attention to the seeds that we have sown?

There are a couple of things to learn from Crazy Quincy. For, in this story we can glean one of God's fundamental laws that governs the globe and gives us a glimpse into God's mind. This law we will discover is noted as early as Genesis in the first chapter and even more specifically within the first 11 verses of the Bible. Yes, on the third day of God's creative exercise. After He had commanded the darkness to roll up on one side and the light to stand shining on the other on the first day. After His Word wrestled the waters of creation to establish a firmament on the second day. It was on the third day when the land and sea are separated that God issues a command to the land to produce seed-bearing plants. By this, God issues the law of sowing and reaping.

THE PROCESS TO YOUR HARVEST

Friends, isn't it interesting that God created seed-bearing plants? For, what this demonstrates to us is that the way that God intended the natural world is not by taking a grown apple tree and cloning and immediately duplicating it, so that it would produce another. Rather, the way that God designed for things to grow in perpetuity is by making a seed that carries all of the DNA of the plant. He locked a potential apple tree within every apple seed. The seed had everything that it needed to be an apple tree within it; however, it was just going to take a process.

That is the point that discourages many of us, because we don't want to go through the process of maturing to reach the harvest that God intends to give us. But in the Law of sowing and reaping or seedtime and harvest, we recognize that the only way to produce fruit is by going through the process. This is where we find the Israelites in the text, going through the process of God giving them their harvest. They have been planted in Babylon and they been preparing for the deliverance, and in this passage we find them praising for their harvest and return from captivity. We can find their steps to getting their harvest in verse 6. These steps mark the process that God wants to use to give you your harvest too!

STEP 1: PLANT IT

The first step that you have to make is to plant it. You cannot expect to receive a harvest if you have not planted anything. As we just noted, God operates through the process of planting seeds. He even used the same strategy in creating the world, for He took His Word and planted it into nothing and said, "let there be light." And light was harvested. He wanted a firmament or sky, and He sowed His Word and said, "Let there be and sky" and He harvested a sky. On the third day, He wanted seed-bearing plants, and He said, "Let there be seed-bearing plants." And He harvested seed-bearing plants. Somebody has caught the pattern. He wanted something and sowed His Word to get the harvest of what He wanted. Then after He said it, He saw it. This was the pattern that He used all six days. He planted His Word, and He received a harvest of that Word.

Let us not think that that was the only time that God used this strategy, for in the New Testament we see that God wants a family, so He takes His Word. John says, "In the beginning was the Word and the Word was with God and the Word was God….and the Word became flesh and dwelt among us." It was by sowing His Son, the Word into the dust and dirt of human flesh that He could harvest the world. This idea is captured in John 3:16, and if you allow me to tweek with my preacher prerogative it would say, "For God so loved the world that He (sowed) His only begotten Son, that whosoever believes in Him shall not perish but have everlasting life." Therefore, He planted His Son to harvest a family, he planted His word to harvest the world. Isn't it interesting that God created seed-bearing plants on the third day, and God got His biggest harvest on the third day when He raised Jesus from the dead!

Planting the Right Seed

If that is how God received a harvest, can you imagine what this system would do for us? You see the reason why God got the harvest that He wanted was due to the fact that He planted the right seed. If we are going to receive a harvest of faith that bears fruits of our deliverance, our dreams, and our destiny, we have to sow the same kind of seeds. Friends, to receive the harvest of faith, you have to sow the seeds of the Word of God. However, if you don't know it, you can't sow it. That's why it is important to know the Word of God. Verse 6 speaks of going out bearing precious seed, but how more precious seed can one sow than the Words of God. The Word of God is so powerful that when it hit nothing it created something. It is so powerful that when it hit Sarah's barren womb, it forced a reaction that brought forth the very chosen people of God. It is so powerful that when it hit dry ground a shoot came out. It is so powerful that when it hit the grave, Life came out and said, "O death where is thy sting, and o grave where is thy victory."

The Word of God is powerful, but we must plant it in our life if we want to receive a harvest of faith that bears fruit of our deliverance, our dreams, and our destiny. God wants to do something so fantastic in your life that He wants you to be like the Israelites and say, "it feels like a dream." God wants to blow your mind with what He has in store for you. He wants to do something so unbelievable in your life that you have to say "pinch me, because I must be dreaming." God wants to make your dreams come true. However, you must first have the fertile ground of dream. Rodgers and Hammerstein put it like this:

"you gotta have a dream,
if you don't have a dream,
how you gonna have a dream come true?"

If God wants to give you a harvest of faith that bears the fruit of your dream, then why not plant the seed of the Word of God in your life to bring it to pass?

What Are You Sowing?

Friends, the way that harvest works is that God has instructed every seed to produce after its kinds. Watermelon seeds make a harvest of watermelon. Grape seeds make a harvest of grapes. Tomato seeds make a harvest of tomatoes. Faith seeds make a harvest of faith. Some may wonder why they have not reaped anything, but if you have not sown anything, it is impossible for you to reap anything. Because in the same way that like produces like, nothing produces nothing. If you want to reap faith, you have to sow words of faith.

One may say that I have been reaping; however, I have not been getting the harvest that I have been sowing. I would suggest like Frank suggested to Quincy, you may need to check the seeds that you are sowing. Are you sowing words of faith and life that showcase the power, purpose, and plan of God? Or are you sowing words of fear and death that showcase the impatience, insecurities, and impotence of you?

Honestly, sometimes we don't get the harvest that we anticipate, because we are sowing words that get the exact opposite of the harvest that we want. Let me give you an example, this week I was headed to assist one of the units at the Boys and Girls Clubs to fill in for missing staff. Someone asked me what I was getting ready to do. The first response that came to my mind was, *I'm about to work with these rowdy kids.* Then the Lord said to me, "what kind of words are you sowing? Are they words of faith and life or words of fear and death?" So, I changed my text message and wrote, "I'm about to help some little kids be great." You see, neither experience had happened yet. The students being loud and disrespectful had not happened nor had they acted well behaved yet. Either way, I was going to have to predict, and my feelings were going to follow my forecast. So, why not believe the best was going to happen rather than the worst? I transformed the seed I was sowing and got a harvest of a good experience working with the students.

Sow Words of Faith

Many of us cannot receive the harvest of faith that produces the fruit of our deliverance, our dreams, and our destiny, because we would rather speak words of fear. It is completely destructive to speak words of fear and death, because they are just a waste of spiritual energy. You see fear really means "finding excuses against relief." The good thing that could happen has not happened, but the bad thing has not either! Why not sow words for the good harvest?

Rather than speak words of faith over the election, some sow words of fear and say that my vote doesn't matter anyway. Rather than speak words of life into someone who is struggling, some speak words of death and say someone really should be encouraging me. If we are going to be the people that God has called for us to be, and if we are to reap the harvest that God has promised for us to have, then we have to sow God's Words of life.

So, I encourage you to sow words of life rather than words of death. Instead of saying that I'm broke, say "He shall supply all of my needs according to His riches in glory." Rather than sow words that express that you are beat-down and tired, say " I am awaiting my renewal, for they that wait upon the Lord shall renew their strength and mount up with wings like eagles they shall run and not be weary, they shall walk and not faint." Rather than state that you are poor and weak declare that "I am the head and not the tail, I am above and not beneath." Rather than sow words of fear saying "I don't deserve any better in life," sow words of faith that say "I am an heir of God and a joint-heir with Jesus Christ." Rather than sow words of death that talk about how sick and hurting you are, speak words of life and declare "that He was wounded for my transgressions, bruised for my iniquities, chastisement of my peace was upon Him and with His stripes, I am healed!!!" Sow words of God, life and faith that produce a harvest of our deliverance, our dreams, and our destiny! To get the harvest that you want you have to plant it!

STEP 2: PREPARE IT

The second step that you have to take is to prepare for it. If you are really anticipating a harvest from God you should prepare for it. You should make room for the harvest that you are expecting. There are some people whom God wants to give the harvest of a promotion to, but you have not even prepared yourself for the elevation. You keep talking about moving higher, you keep talking about getting more playtime, you keep talking about getting a new job, but you have not done anything to prepare for your position. Friends, if you want to receive God's harvest, you have to prepare for it. Although you may not be in the top position, you need to start thinking about the decisions that you would make if you got it. Even though you are not free from whatever is binding you, you need to go ahead and start thinking about what you are going to do when you get free so that you don't get bound again!

That is the same position that Israelites find themselves in within our text. They have been waiting patiently for 70 years to escape the clutches of Babylonian rule, and now God is freeing them, returning their captivity.

They are prepared to receive their harvest, but the reason that they are prepared to receive it is because they know what they did to prepare the harvest. They knew that their deliverance was going to happen, because it was based on a Word that came from God through the mouth of Jeremiah. However, although the word was planted it had to be prepared and watered.

Watering Your Harvest

So, there they were in Babylon just waiting on the seed to bear fruit. There was nothing much more that they could do but wait. As they waited, tears of worry filled their eyes as they thought about how they didn't want for their children to be raised in this situation. Tears of worry welled up when they thought of how many mistakes that they had made. Tears of worry rolled down their faces as they asked God for one more chance. But they knew that there was a word planted in the fertile ground of their life. Even though it didn't seem like, it didn't feel like, and it didn't look like it, God had planted a word in them saying, "trouble don't last always. For my anger is but a moment, and in my favor is life, weeping may endure for a night, but joy comes in the morning." So, these tears that hit the ground were not just tears of worrying, but they were tears of worship, and God sent me by to tell someone that "the tears that you have been shedding are watering your harvest." The tears you are shedding for your wayward child are watering the harvest of his return. The tears that you are shedding for that broken relationship are watering the harvest for a new fruitful and life giving relationship. The tears that you are shedding because of your past failure are watering the harvest of your future success!

Waiting on Your Harvest

Even though you find yourself in Babylon, and truth be told, you got yourself into the mess, God has made a commitment to get you out! The only challenge is that you have to wait on Him. This is the hardest part of getting a harvest--waiting for it to come. However, there is good news. God is not unpredictable like common crops, God is never late, rarely early, but always right on time! So, all you have to do is do your part and be faithful. God is going to do His part.

The image in our passage that best shows this is in verse 4 when the Psalmist declares "return our captivity, Lord, like the streams of the south." The casual reader might have missed this, but what the author is conveying is how Israel was normally a desert. However, after the winter, when the ice caps melted on the top of the mountains, the waters would begin to flow from the mountains in the north all the way to the streams of the south. Preacher, what are you saying? The people in the South really didn't know what caused the streams to come; however, they knew that something was working for them that they could not explain. They knew that something was happening that was out of their control, and if they waited long enough they were going to get renewed. Similarly, God is saying, "just because you cannot see me work does not mean that I am not working. Just because I'm not showing my work does not mean that I'm not doing it." Just like the seed, although it's in the ground it is not dormant. As a matter of fact, the seed does its most amazing growth under the ground when it cannot be seen! God says, "Out of your sight, does not mean out of my mind." That's how God is working for your harvest of faith that produces your deliverance, your dream, and your destiny. You just have to sow all of your faith into Him!

Jesus' Harvest

This is the how Jesus prepared His harvest. He sowed all of His faith into God. His faith dripped down his brow through beads of sweat. His faith flowed from His veins with drops of blood. His faith rolled down His cheek in shed tears. He sowed all of His faith to the point of death. That's why,

"When I survey the wondrous cross
on which the prince of glory died,
my richest gains I count as lost
and poor contempt on all my pride.
Were the whole realm of nature mine
That were a present far too small

Love so amazing, love so divine,
Demands my life, my heart, my all."

But the wonder of the cross is not even seen on the cross. As a matter of fact, the wonder that is seen can actually not be seen, because as Jesus had sowed all of his faith and self into God, He did so as a seed. Because the Scriptures declare that "unless a seed falls to the ground and dies it cannot bear fruit." So, after He planted all of His faith and He planted Himself (the Word of God) as a seed, God was working it out. For all the sweat that poured, God was working it out. For all the blood that was shed, God was working it out. For all of the tears that were cried, God was working it out. This captures Paul's idea that "our current suffering is working for us a far more eternal weight of glory."

So, as Jesus poured His all into God and sowed all He could, God began to work on His harvest of faith producing fruit of His deliverance, His dreams, and His destiny. On Friday night, God was working it out. On Saturday night, God was working it out, but early Sunday morning, God gave Jesus His harvest and raised Him from the dead! Hallelujah.

Due Season!

Jesus is our example, so "don't grow weary in well doing, for in due season you will reap if you don't faint!" That verse is powerful for the believer, because it shows that for those who expect their harvest there are actually five seasons and not just four, because for the believer, there is not just a winter, spring summer, and fall, but there is also a "due" season.

Let me encourage you. Your due season is on the way. Don't faint now. Don't give up. Your due season is coming. "Wait I say on the Lord and be of good courage and He will strengthen your heart!" Keep pressing. Keep pressing. Your harvest is coming! God has not forgotten you. I don't know about you but I've got to get my harvest!

STEP 3: PRAISE FOR IT!

The last thing that I want to share with you in this passage is the final step to getting your harvest. After you plant, after you prepare, you have to praise. For this group of people is the same group that said in Psalm 137 that "we hung up our harps on the willows of Babylon, because they asked for us to sing a song, and we responded how can we sing the Lord's song in a strange land." But now, this same group of people has a different testimony. This group had dusted off their harps and declared that "I must give God some praise, because He has brought us our harvest."

This group praises Him so crazily that the heathen jumps in their praise party and says "the Lord had done great things for them!" We should come in here and give God praise so great that the heathen gets jealous of our praise. They should look in here and say "their God is so great, I want to praise Him for the wonderful things in their life." I don't know about you, but I refuse to let a heathen out-praise me. I refuse to let someone who does not know how good God has been out praise. I refuse to let someone who has never gotten a harvest from God to out praise me.

Why? Because the harvest shows that our God is faithful. It shows that our God keeps His promises. He's not a man that He should lie. Therefore, I can praise Him that He has been faithful in my life, but I can also praise Him on credit for the harvest that He has promised me. I'm going to praise for Him for the deliverance that He brought in my life through His Son Jesus. I'm going to praise Him for the dream business, job, relationship, and success that He promised me. I'm going to praise Him for the destiny that "eye has not seen nor ear hear nor that has entered into the heart of man!"

Can I praise Him for me right now? In the words of Richard Smallwood, Lord I thank you,

"For every mountain, you brought me over
For every trial you've seen me through
For every blessing, Hallelujah
For this I give you praise!"

Church, Andre Crouch put it this way,

"I thank Him for my valleys
and for the storms He brought me through
For if I never had a problem,
I wouldn't know that God could solve them.
I would not know what faith in God's Word would do!"

I thank Him for the harvest, and I thank Him for the draught that taught me to appreciate the harvest.

I thank Him for my harvest that has come and is coming! Amen.

FROM THE FRAT HOUSE TO THE CHURCH HOUSE

This forthcoming book is an autobiographical anthology of Jeremy L. Williams' messages while he was a student at Vanderbilt University. It captures different modes, environments, and levels of growth in his ministry. It also takes into consideration the challenges of being a student while also being preacher. In this excerpt we will share part a message from Jeremy's junior year in college entitled "#Follow Jesus."

~~~~~~

#FOLLOWJESUS

24 But Thomas (who was called the Twin), one of the twelve, was not with them when Jesus came. 25 So the other disciples told him, 'We have seen the Lord.' But he said to them, 'Unless I see the mark of the nails in his hands, and put my finger in the mark of the nails and my hand in his side, I will not believe.'

26 A week later his disciples were again in the house, and Thomas was with them. Although the doors were shut, Jesus came and stood among them and said, 'Peace be with you.' 27 Then he said to Thomas, 'Put your finger here and see my hands. Reach out your hand and put it in my side. Do not doubt but believe.' 28 Thomas answered him, 'My Lord and my God!' 29 Jesus said to him, 'Have you believed because you have seen me? Blessed are those who have not seen and yet have come to believe.'

Though these words do not appear in this passage, they immediately reverberate in the memory of the Bible reader. For, although this passage only names one disciple it infers the presence of a Peter who was fishing with his brother, Andrew, in Capernaum when one Gospel writer records that Jesus strolls on the shore and says with sanguine serenity "Follow me and I will make you fishers of men." Yes. In this passage we see on the margins, those boisterous and manipulative Sons of Thunder, who according to another Evangelist did not fret to drop their nets and let the *logos* of this Stranger set them in a different path with His inoculated imperative to "Follow me."

This was the call that was taken by tax collector Matthew, tried by terrorist Simon, built on by the betrayer Judas, and it is this call that is now being dug into by Doubting Thomas. I can hear Thomas asking on this week after Easter when Jesus is out of sight, "What does it mean to follow Jesus in world where he is missing? What does it mean to follow Jesus when good people are being executed for telling the truth? What does it mean to follow Jesus in a world where people don't like him and they definitely don't like you? What does it mean to follow Jesus when tsunamis and tornadoes are killing people in our back yards? What does it mean to follow Jesus when racism fills the media as birthers beg for the President Barack's birth certificate? What does it mean to follow Jesus as a young adult in the

21ˢᵗ century? What does it mean to follow Jesus when everyone in my friend group practices unsafe sexual behaviors? What does it mean to follow Jesus when my mind is telling me no, but my body is telling me yes? What does it mean to follow Jesus?"

JESUS IS ON THE MAINLINE/ONLINE

These are the questions that should perennially plague the believer, and I hate to tell you this, but I can't honestly answer them completely myself. However, we can definitely glean a framework from the text to help us out, but we can also find help in another place—social media. Specifically, we can look at Twitter and later facebook. I know you have a twitter or facebook, so there's no need for you to look like I'm out of order. I just would like to engage the metaphor momentarily. The seasoned saints ought not get disenchanted either, because this not the first time someone has used a popular communication device to explain a relationship with God.

Let me give you an example, because you don't believe me. I know y'all don't sing this up here, but back in Alabama we have a song, "Jesus is on the mainline, tell him what you want." However, this song sounded good and made me feel good singing it, but I could not connect with it, because I've never used a party line before. As a matter of fact, I still don't know what a mainline is outside of

Jesus being on it; however, a more contemporary version would be Jesus has unlimited minutes tell Him what you want, His texts don't run out so you can tell Him what you want, He's always online on facebook so you can tell Him what you want, you just

Skype Him up and tell Him what you want...

NOTES

NOTES

ABOUT THE AUTHOR

The Rev'd Jeremy L. Williams is a native of Huntsville, Alabama where he grew up at Acklin C.M.E. Church. He was ordained in the North Central Alabama Region of the Christian Methodist Episcopal Church in 2011. At a young age the fire of God lit his soul ablaze with an inescapable call that left him answerable to none other than the voice of the Almighty. He responded affirmatively to that divine summons and has been proclaiming the good news of Jesus Christ for over 10 years. His ministry has carried him to various venues throughout North Alabama, Middle Tennessee, Louisville, Kentucky, and Chicago, Illinois. He has hosted conferences, preached revivals, and developed workshops for the expansion of the Kingdom of God with a special focus youth and young adults. He has visited Morocco and China to explore the impact of religion and culture on society. Recently, he was inducted into the National Academy of Preachers.

His ministry as an ambassador of Jesus Christ is to make people aware of who they are in Christ, and more importantly, who Christ is in them. Upon graduating from Vanderbilt University with Highest Honors in Religious Studies, he was appointed as the Conference Evangelist for the North Central Alabama Region of the C.M.E. Church. He also deferred his admission to Yale Divinity School for a year, as he serves his community in a uniquely created role at the Boys and Girls Clubs of North Alabama. He also just launched his company *Dream Better Dreams*, whose mission is to "create the hope, invigorate the potential, and stimulate the understanding of people in order to assist them in achieving their dreams." Last, but certainly not least, he is a proud member of that most Noble Clan of Achievers, none other than Kappa Alpha Psi where he serves internationally as the 2nd Vice President of the entire Fraternity.

Made in the USA
Charleston, SC
09 June 2013